SCOTTISH-FLEMISH LINKS

1100 - 1850

By David Dobson

CLEARFIELD

Copyright © 2025
by David Dobson
All Rights Reserved

Published for Clearfield Company by
Genealogical Publishing Company
Baltimore, Maryland
2025

ISBN: 9780806360690

SCOTTISH-FLEMISH LINKS, 1100 – 1850

INTRODUCTION

The Flemish connections with Scotland can be traced from the reign of King David II, who encouraged settlement by Norman-Flemish families from England in the early twelfth century. These pioneer settlers were generally granted land especially in Upper Lanarkshire, Moray, and Lothian. Some Flemings converted their property names into surnames, for example, Crawford and Murray. In Lanarkshire, several towns are named after their Flemish founders, including Symington, named after Simon; and Lambington, named after Lambin. Freskin the Fleming was granted lands in Moray, and his family was called 'de Moravia,' which became Murray, while the head of the family became Lord Sutherland in 1214.

These men had links to Flanders, whose textile manufacturing had made it the most industrialized region of northern Europe. Flanders was heavily dependent on England and Scotland for wool. The economy of the abbeys which were being established in Scotland heavily depended on the export of wool through ports such as Berwick-on-Tweed, Leith, Perth and Dundee. Flemish merchants and craftsmen settled in such towns, especially in the Canongait. Burghs were established, generally on Scotland's east coast, to encourage trade with Flanders, while castles and churches were constructed, often using Flemish craftsmen. Mainard the Fleming was employed to develop burghs such as Berwick-on-Tweed and St. Andrews.

Flemish craftsmen were encouraged to settle and train local people in the latest techniques for weaving textiles; in fact, in 1601 Claus Lossier, a shearer, Cornelis Dermis, a weaver, and Henri de Turk, a clothmaker, were sent to Dundee for that purpose. The volume of trade between Scotland and Flanders during the Early Modern Period generated an expansion of ships and seamen in both Flanders and Scotland. Scotland exported food, such as fish, and raw materials, especially wool, hides, and coal, while manufactured goods and textiles were sent from Flanders to Scotland.

In Flanders, the city of Bruges was the Staple Port for Scottish trade in the medieval period; later, it became Veere in Zealand. Bruges and Antwerp attracted Scottish merchants and craftsmen; however, from the late sixteenth until the early nineteenth century, the majority of the Scots in Flanders were soldiers. The Scotch Brigade fought in the Low Countries against the Spanish, who were attempting to keep the Dutch and Flemish in the Spanish Empire. Later Scottish regiments of the British Army fought against the French through the Battle of Waterloo in 1815.

David Dobson, Dundee, 2025

SOME SHIPPING LINKS

American Union of Dunkirk, a privateer, with 6 guns and 19 crew, was captured by the Iphigenia in 1781. [SM.43.442]

On 18 May 1632, two 'freebooters' from West Flanders stole a Flemish hoy and some Dutch vessels at anchor in the Firth of Forth. [RPCS.IV.488]

'The St John of Bruges' alias St Jan van Brogge, was at Peterhead, Aberdeenshire, in December 1673. [NRS.E75.58.6]

REFERENCES

AB Aberdeen before 1800, [East Linton, 2002]

ABR Aberdeen Burgess Roll

ACB Acta Curiae Admirallatus Scotiae, 1557-1561 [Edinburgh, 1937]

ACA Aberdeen City Archives

ACL Aberdeen Council Letters, [Oxford, 1942-1961]

AGC Aberdeen Guild Court Records, 1437-1468, [Edinburgh 2005]

AJ Aberdeen Journal, series

AMW Accounts of the Master of Works, [Edinburgh, 1957]

AS   Antwerpen Stadarchief,Poortersboeken, Vierschaar, [142/42; 144/36; 152/50; 152/13]

ASW Aberdeen Shore Works, [Aberdeen, 1972]

ATS Accounts of the Lord High Treasurer of Scotland, [Edinburgh, 1877]

BM Book of Mackay

BR Bibliotheque Royale, Brussels

CBR Canongait Burgess Roll, [Edinburgh 1898]

CDS Calendar of Documents, Scotland, [Edinburgh, 1867]

CSP.Scot. Calendar of State Papers, Scotland, 1547-1603, [Edinburgh 1903]

CSP. Foreign Calendar of State Papers, XXII, [London, 1936]

DR Dunfermline Burgh Records, [Edinburgh, 1917]

DD The Darien Disaster, [London, 1978]

DP Darien Papers, [Edinburgh, 1849]

DWCB David Wedderburn's Compt Buik,

ERS Exchequer Rolls of Scotland

EUL Edinburgh University Library

F Fasti Ecclesianae Scoticanae, [Edinburgh]

GAR Rotterdam Archives

GM The Gentleman's Magazine, series, [London]

HGH History of the Gordon Highlanders, [Edinburgh, 1901]

H78. A History of the 2nd Battalion of the 78th Foot, 1804-1816, [Edinburgh, 2011]

JCTP. Journal of the Committee for Trade and Plantations, series, [London]

JP The Jacobite Peerage, [Edinburgh, 1904]

JTC Journal of Thomas Cunningham of Campveere 1640-1654, [Edinburgh, 1927]

KS The Kingdom of the Scots, [London, 1973]

LAH Ledger of Andrew Haliburton, [Edinburgh,1867]

LC Calendar of the Laing Charters, 854-1837, [Edinburgh, 1848]

LGL Letters of George Lockhart of Carnwath, [Edinburgh, 1989]

LJV The Letters of James V, [Edinburgh, 1954]

LMR Leiden Marriage Register

LT The Linen Trade, [Dundee, 18

MSC. Misc. of the Spalding Club, [Aberdeen, 1940]

NLS National Library of Scotland

NRAS National Register of Archives in Scotland

NRS National Records of Scotland

PGB Perth Guildry Book, 1452-1601, [Edinburgh]

PJD People's Journal, Dundee, series,

PKA Perth and Kinross Archives

PL The Port of Leith, [Edinburgh, 1991]

PS Painters in Scotland, 1301-1700, [Edinburgh, 1978]

RAK Copenhagen Archives

RPCS Register of the Privy Council of Scotland

RPSS Register of the Privy Seal of Scotland

SA Antwerpen Archives

SAA Antwerpen Poorersboekens

SB The Scots Brigade in Holland, [Edinburgh, 1899]

SFP Scotland and the Flemish People, [Edinburgh, 2019]

SHS Scottish History Society, Edinburgh

SHR Scottish Historical Review, series

SJC Selected Justiciary Cases 1624-1650, [Edinburgh, 1972]

SLC Scotland and the Low Countries, 1124-1994.

SNQ Scottish Notes and Queries, series

SP The Scots Peerage, [Edinburgh, 1904]

SSN The Scottish Staple at Veere, [London, 1910]

STR Sound Toll Register, Danish Archives

TNA The National Archives, London

WBA West Brabant Archives, Belgium

WC Weekly Chronicle, series

WCB David Wedderburne's Compt Buik, 1587-1630, [Edinburgh, 1898]

XEBR Extracts from the Edinburgh Burgh Records, series, [Edinburgh]

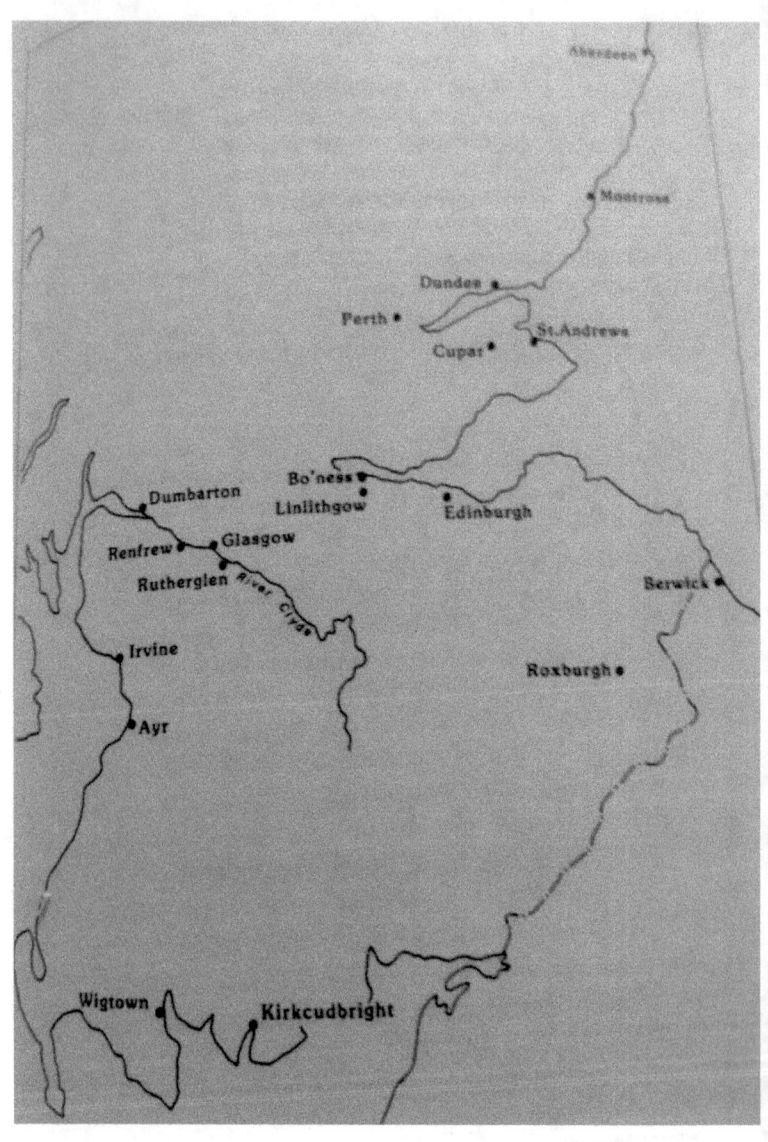

Map of Central Scotland, showing location of Glasgow

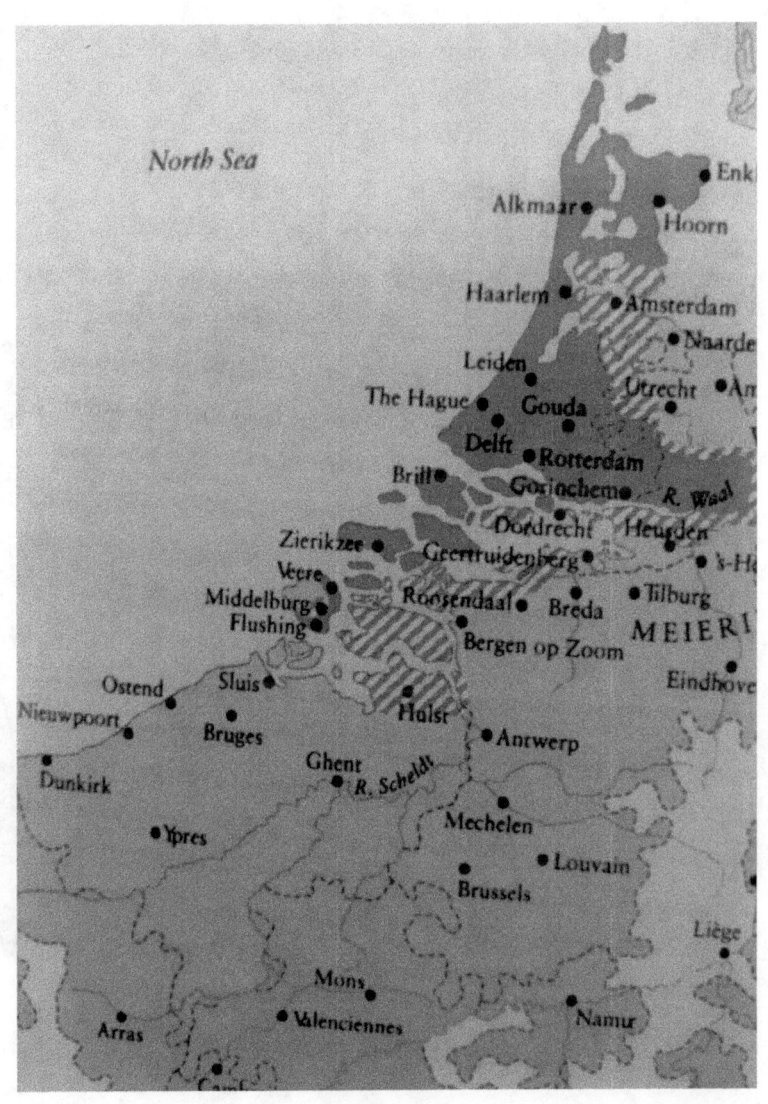

Map of Low Countries

Montrose Harbor and the Horologe Hill
Painted by Henrietta Ouchterlony, ca. 1810

ABERCROMBY, G., in Brussels, a letter in 1792. [NRS.NRAS.3955.20.1.83]

ADAM, ROBERT, in Brussels, a letter dated in November 1754, to his sister Helen Adam; a letter from Doornik [Tournai] dated 12 November 1754, [NRS.GD18.4749]; a letter from Antwerpen [Antwerp] dated 1757. [NRS.GD18.4748/4845/4857]

ADORNES, ANSELM, born 1424 in Brugge [Bruges], a merchant moved to Scotland in 1468, was knighted there and became a member of the Scottish Privy Council, he went on pilgrimage to the Holy Land from 1470 to 1471, then via Bruges to Scotland, King James III granted him land and promoted him to Conservator of the privileges of Scottish merchants in Burgundy, he returned to Bruges in 1472. [SFP.34]

ADRIAENS, JENNEKE, from Flanders, married Pieter Jansz, [Peter Johnson] a widower from Aberdeen, in Dordrecht on 4 December 1583. [Dordrecht Marriage Register]

AGNEW, ANDREW, in the garrison at Kortrijk, [Courtrai] son of Sir James Agnew of Lochnaw, a letter dated 2 March 1711. [NRS.GD154.677]

AGNEW, Sir ANDREW, was requested to forward muster rolls to Brussels on 24 June 1745. [NRS.GD154.638]

AGNEW, GEORGE, formerly an Ensign of Colonel Douglas's Regiment of Foot in Flanders, later a Lieutenant of the Scots Company at Darien, Panama, around 1698-1699, testament confirmed with the Commissariat of Edinburgh on 4 February 1708. [NRS]

AIKEN, JOHN, [Jan Eycken], from Perth [St Jansstad], a soldier under Captain Arians, married Tanneken Jans from Steken in Vlaanderen [Flanders], in Rotterdam on 1 November 1601. [Rotterdam Marriage Register]

AIKMAN, GEORGE, master of the John of Aberdeen was captured by two privateers, masters Pieter Careu and Pieter de Rudder from Duinkerken [Dunkirk] in 1649, and taken to Duinkerken [Dunkirk]. [ACL.3.131][JTC.241]

AIR, ALEXANDER, a soldier in Captain L'Amy's Company of the Scots Brigade, [De Schotse Brigade] married Joanna Tubbings, in Hulst on 23 April 1659. [SB]

AIR, GEORGE, [Joris Aer] a soldier in Captain Mowbray's Company of the Scots Brigade, [De Schotse Brigade] married Margriet Jans from Eindhoven on 9 July 1630. [SB]

AITCHISON, JOHN, the Customar of Newhaven of Preston, was captured and imprisoned by the Flemings in 1545. [ERS.18.68]

ALEXANDER, ELIZABETH, daughter of John Alexander a soldier of Colonel Dalet's Company of the Scots Brigade, [De Schotse Brigade] ,and his wife Janet Cockburn, was baptised in Yperen [Ypres] on16 March 1736. [SB]

ALEXANDER, JAMES, a Scot, was married in Bergen op Zoom on 18 October1680. [WBA]

ALEXANDER, JAMES, son of Major James Alexander and his wife Jean Elphinstone, was baptised in Doornik [Tournai] on 31 January 1713 [SB]

ALEXANDER, JOHN, a soldier, married Janet Stot, in Yperen [Ypres] on 5 July 1735. [SB]

ALEXANDER, RICHARD, born 1615, was granted a licence to travel to Vlaanderen [Flanders] in 1635. [TNA.E157.20]

ALISON, JOHN, in Vlaanderen [Flanders], a deed dated 1686. [NRS.RD2.66.99]

ALLAN, JAMES, son of William Allan, a soldier of Major Alexander's Company in the Scots Brigade, [De Schotse Brigade] ,was baptised in Doornik [Tournai] in 1714. [SB]

ALLAN, JAMES, a Sergeant of Captain James Lockhart's Company of General Coalzier's Regiment at Namur, testament confirmed on 20 May 1742. [NRS]

ALLAN, JOHN, master of the Martin of Aberdour trading between Kirkcaldy in Fife and Brugge [Bruges] in 1681. [NRS.E74.9.10]

ALLAN, WILLIAM, master of the Grizel, bound from Aberdeen to Dunkirk in 1749. [NRS.AC8.724]

ALLANG, ANDREW, master of the Blimzeland arrived in Dundee from Vlaanderen [Flanders] in 1631. [DSL]

ALLARDYCE, HENRY, a prisoner in Edinburgh Tolbooth, was released to go as a soldier to Flanders on 22 February 1621. [RPCS.XII.431]

ANDERSON, ALEXANDER, master of the Robert of Montrose arrived from Duinkirken [Dunkirk] in June 1686. [NRS.E72.16.15]

ANDERSON, GILBERT, [Gilbert Andriesz.], a Scot, married Maycken Beuffkens from Roussy in Vlaanderen [Flanders] in Leiden on 9 February 1585. [Leiden Marriage Register]

ANDERSON, JOHN, a merchant from Scotland, was admitted as a burgess of Antwerpen [Antwerp] in 1539. [SA.Antwerpen Poorterboek]

ANDERSON, LAURENCE, in Leith, was accused of importing false coinage from Flanders on 6 October 1517. [RPSS.I.2942]

ANDERSON, MATTHEW, master of the Lyon of Kirkcaldy in Fife bound for Oostende [Ostend] on 25 April 1681, returned via Brugge [Bruges] [NRS.E29.9]

ANDERSON, PATRICK, a Jesuit priest, who was taken from Edinburgh Tolbooth and put on board a ship bound for Vlanderen [Flanders] or France in February 1621. [RPCS.XII.419]

ANDERSON, WILLIAM, master of the David of Kirkcaldy, from Brugge [Bruges] to Kirkcaldy in 1683. [NRS.E72.9.15]

ANDREWS, GEORGE, a soldier of Lieutenant Colonel Sir Andrew Agnew's Company of the Scots Brigade, [De Schotse Brigade], in Brugge [Bruges] on 13 June 1745. [NRS.GD154.636]

ANDREWS, JAMES, a Scot, was married in Bergen op Zoom on 2 October 1715. [WBA]

ANDREWS, PETER, from Edinburgh, married Phillipijntge Claes from Brussels, in Rotterdam on 26 October 1603. [Rotterdam Marriage Register]

ANGUS, JAMES, a skipper and baillie of Burntisland in Fife, master of the James of Burntisland bound from Kirkcaldy in Fife for Oostende [Ostend] in August 1670. [NRS.E72.9.4]

ANGUS, JOHN, master of the Hope of Burntisland in Fife, arrived in Kirkcaldy in Fife from Ostend on 28 March 1670. [NRS.E2.9]

ANGUS, Earl of, his Regiment was bound to Flanders on 21 February 1704, vouchers. [NRS.E95.48]

ARAZ, MATTHIEU DE, [Matthew Arras], possibly a tapestry maker from Arras in Flanders, was in Scotland in 1312. [FSP.61]

ARBUCKLE, JOHN, son of Hugh Arbuckle, a soldier of Captain Watson's company, and his wife Elisabeth Vasar, was baptised in Namur on 17 July 1737. [SB3BR]

ARBUTHNOTT, JAMES, a Sergeant of Lieutenant Colonel Sir Andrew Agnew's Company of the Scots Brigade, [De Schotse Brigade] in Brugge [Bruges] on 13 June 1745. [NRS.GD154.636]

ARCHER, JAMES, SJ, from Kilkenny, a chaplain to Sir William Stanley's Regiment in Flanders around 1587. [IS.30.122]

ARGETT, Captain, master of the Reynard of Duinkerken [Dunkirk] which was sold in Leith on 12 August 1704. [NRS.AC7.11]

ARMSTRONG, MATTHEW, a soldier who was granted a licence to travel to Vlaanderen [Flanders] in 1631. [TNA.E157.15]

AUCHENCLOSS, ROBERT, a Scot, was married in Bergen op Zoom on 30 September 1685. [WBA]

AUSTIN, ROBERT, a Scot, was married in Bergen op Zoom on 22 January 1695. [WBA]

AYSON, ALEXANDER, from Flanders aboard the Flower bound for Scotland in 1495. [ERS.X.535]

BAILLIE, GEORGE, master of the George of Dundee from Vlanderen [Flanders] to Dundee in 1616. [DSL]

BAILLIE, JOHN, a Lieutenant Colonel of Colonel Buchan's Regiment in Vlaanderen [Flanders] before 1697, enlisted with the 'Company of Scotland trading to Africa and the Indies', sailed from Leith aboard the Rising Sun bound for Darien, Panama, in 1699, died there in February 1700. [APS.XIV.app.127]

BAILLIE, WILLIAM, of Hardington, a Captain of Colonel Buchan's Regiment in Vlaanderen [Flanders], married Anna Johnston, third daughter of the late James Johnston of Schens, an ante-nuptial marriage contract dated on 27 February 1697. [NRS.RH9.7.192]

BAILLIE, WILLIAM, a Scot, was married in Bergen op Zoom on 12 January 1702. [WBA]

BAILLIE, WILLIAM, the younger of Backbie, formerly a Cornet in Lord Carmichael's Regiment of Dragoons in Flanders, later in the service of the Darien Company in Panama, testament confirmed with the Commissariat of Edinburgh on 18 September 1707. [NRS]

BAIN, DONALD, a soldier in Captain Mackay's Company of the Scots Brigade, [De Schotse Brigade], married Elizabeth Smith, a widow, in Yperen [Ypres] on 8 August 1778. [SB]

BAIRD, JAMES, in Antwerpen [Antwerp] a letter dated 1794. [NRS.GD24.1.447A.21]

BAKER, RICHARD, a soldier of Lieutenant Colonel Sir Andrew Agnew's Company of the Scots Brigade, [De Schotse Brigade], in Brugge [Bruges] on 13 June 1745. [NRS.GD154.636]

BALDWYN, probably Flemish, emigrated from Yorkshire, England, to Scotland after 1147, settled at Biggar in Lanarkshire, by 1154, later Sheriff of Lanark and Clydesdale in 1159. [SFP]

BALDWYN, a Flemish lorimer, was granted a toft in Perth in 1150s. [PKA]

BALFOUR, ANDREW, a merchant in Flanders in 1538. [RPSS.2.2539]

BALFOUR, B., in Breda, Brabant, letters dated 1683. [NRS.GD306.1.9001/3]

BALFOUR, JOHN, a mariner in Leith, was aboard the John of Leith bound from Vlaanderen [Flanders] to Leith in September 1633. [SJC.I.206]

BALFOUR, NINIAN, master of the Clayge Coist of Dundee from Vlaanderen [Flanders] to Dundee in October 1616, and to Aberdeen in November 1621. [DSL][ASW.111]

BALLENTINE, GEORGE, [Joris Ballentijn], a confectioner from Edinburgh, a servant of Cornelis Engelsz. van Gaesbeck, married Anna Bultings from Gent [Gand] in Leiden on 16 December 1617. [Leiden Marriage Register]; and was admitted as a citizen of Leiden on 18 May 1618. [Leiden Citizenship Book, II.112]

BALLANTYNE, JAMES, a Lieutenant of the Earl of Angus's Regiment of Foot in Vlaanderen [Flanders], was admitted as a burgess and guilds-brother of Ayr on 11 January 1692. [Ayr Burgess Register]

BALVAIRD, JAMES, master of the James of Kirkcaldy from Kirkcaldy in Fife bound for Oostende [Ostend] in January 1671. [NRS.E729.5]

BALZART, JOHN, in Leith, was accused of importing false coinage from Flanders on 6 October 1517. [RPSS.I.2942]

BANKO, JOHN, a Flemish weaver, was permitted to settle in Scotland and follow his trade there in 1587. [SFP.63]

BARFOOT, CLEOFAS, master of the Jacob van Brugge [James of Bruges], arrived in Leith from Brugge with a cargo of iron, iron-pots, brass, raisins, flax, sugar, candy, aniseed, madder and figs, in 1666. [NRS.E72.15.2]

BARR, JOHN, master of the Sophia of Leith from Prestonpans in Midlothian to Duinkerken [Dunkirk], in December 1681. [NRS.E72.21.4]

BARR, ROBERT, a manufacturer in Paisley in Renfrewshire, trading with Antwerpen [Antwerp] from 1771 until 1800. [NRS.CS96.3432]

BARRON, ELIZABETH, daughter of George Barron, a soldier in Major Gordon's Company of the Scots Brigade, [De Schotse Brigade], and Jean Law, his wife, was baptized in Yperen [Ypres] on 1 April 1734, also daughter Anna Barron, who was baptised there on 22 February 1737. [SB]

BARTHOLMEW, a Fleming, was a mason at Edinburgh Castle in 1539. [AMW.11.399]

BARTHOLEMEW, JOHN, from Aberdeen, married Catrijn Pieter from] Antwerpen [Antwerp] in Gouda on 13 May 1590. [Gouda Marriage Register]

BARTON, Sir ANDREW, born 1466 in Leith son of John Barton a shipmaster, Andrew Barton was a shipmaster trading with Flemish ports according to Halyburton's Ledger, in 1485 and in 1501 he was granted Letters of Marque by King James IV to attack Portuguese ships in revenge for Portuguese attacks on his father's ship, in 1509 Andrew captured the Estevan van Antwerpen master Pieter Lampen, however in 1511 Barton, then master of the Unicorn was captured and executed by the English.

BARTON, ROBERT, was reimbursed expenses incurred in Flanders, when aboard George Patterson's ship from Leith in 1504. [ATS]

BAXTER, FRANCIS, a Scot, was married in Bergen op Zoom,Brabant, on 26 January 1650. [WBA]

BEATTIE, HENRY, the younger, was captured when his ship was taken by the Lion of Dunkirk. His ransom had not been paid by 1714. [NRS.HCAS.AC8.176]

BEATTIE, ROBERT, master of the John and Christian of Montrose from Montrose in Angus to Duinkerken [Dunkirk] in December 1742; master of the Margaret of Montrose trading between Duinkerken and Montrose in 1748, a smuggler. [NRS.CE53.1.4]; master of the Pretty Jean of Montrose trading between Perth and Duinkerken [Dunkirk] in 1754. [NRS.E504.27.3// 24.1]

BEEST, F. V. a letter to Major Coult in Edinburgh Castle a letter with news of his journey to Flanders and of a siege, dated 26 August 1709. [NRS.GD26.9.437]

BEGG, ALEXANDER, a Scot, was married in Bergen op Zoom, Brabant, on 29 July 1733. [WBA]

BELL, GREGORY, master of the the Blessing of Leith, was captured by Dunkirk privateers when bound from Leith to Zeeland in May 1645. [TNA.HCA.13.60]

BEL, THOMAS, a soldier of Captain Moodies' Company of Major General McKay's Regiment aboard ship in Leith bound for Vlaanderen [Flanders], was taken ashore to be imprisoned in Canongait Tolbooth on order of the Privy Council. [RPCA.XVI.1.127]

BENNY, FRANCOIS, a hotel-keeper in Brussels, versus the Earl of Buchan, a Decreet of Adjudication dated in July 1837. [NRS.CS46.1837.7.221]

BEROWALD, a Fleming, was granted the lands of Innes and of Nether Urquhart by King Malcolm IV in 1160. [SFP]

BERRY, DAVID, master of the Providence of Kinghorn from Anstruther in Fife to Duinkerken [Dunkirk] in April 1749. [NRS.E504.3.1]

BEVERIDGE, HENRY, master of the Pelican of Kirkcaldy trading between Kirkcaldy in Fife and Oostende [Ostend] in 1673. [NRS.E72.9.8]

BIGGART, JOHN, in Perth, a deed dated 1593. [NRS.RD59.8.5.2188]

BISCHOP, GABRIEL, a Flemish manufacturer of broadcloth and stuff, and his family, moved from Norwich, England, to Edinburgh in 1601. [EBR]

BISCHOP, AGNES, wife of William Kemp a merchant burgess of Edinburgh, in 1614. [NRS.GD3.2.25.4]

BISSET, WILLIAM, and Company, flax weavers in Leven in Fife, trading with Antwerpen [Antwerp] in 1837. [NRS.CS96.4686]

BLABRE, DAVID, from Aberdeen, then in Vlaanderen [Flanders], expected to return on 10 July 1540. [ACR.810]

BLACKADDER, JOHN, a Captain of Colonel James Ferguson's Regiment in Vlaanderen [Flanders], a deed dated in 1696. [NRS.RD2.29.838]

BLACKHALL, ROBERT, a merchant from Scotland, was admitted as a burgess of Antwerpen [Antwerp] in 1544. [SA.Antwerpen, Poorterboek]

BLAIR, ALEXANDER, a soldier of Lieutenant Colonel Sir Andrew Agnew's Company of the Scots Brigade, [De Schotse Brigade], in Brugge [Bruges] on 13 June 1745. [NRS.GD154.636]

BLANTYRE, Lord, was buried in Brussel in 1830 by William Drury the minister of St George's. [NRS.NRAS.3432.47]

BLOOK, THOMAS, master of the Maria van Brugge, [Mary of Bruges], at Bo'ness in West Lothian with a cargo of coal bound for Vlaanderen [Flanders] in August 1666. [NRS.E72.5]

BLYTH, GEORGE, master of the Christian of Kirkcaldy trading between Kirkcaldy in Fife and Duinkerken [Dunkirk] also Brugge [Bruges] between 1671 to 1681. [NRS.E72.9.8/9/10/11]

BLYTH, WILLIAM, master of the Gift of God from Vlaanderen [Flanders] to Dundee in 1614. [DSL]

BOGENA, HINNING HENRICKS, master of the Freundschoff van Ostende, trading between Oostende [Ostend] and Dundee in 1782. [NRS.E504.11.9]

BOSWELL, ['Boiseul?'], DAVID, Captain of the Scottish infantry in Colonel Edward Preston's Regiment in

Vlaanderen [Flanders] in 1583, the Council of Bruges agreed to pay them. [NRS.GD226.18.8]

BOSWELL, JOHN, a bailie of Kinghorn in Fife, was licensed to sail to Ostend in Flanders on business, in February 1665. [RPCS.11.30]

BOSWELL, THOMAS, master of the Margaret of Kirkcaldy in Fife trading between Brugge [Bruges] and Kirkcaldy on 25 July 1683. [NRS.E72.9.14]

BOYACK, ROBERT, a surgeon in Brussels, a sasine dated 1768. [NRS.RS35.22.434]

BOYCE, THOMAS, a shipmaster trading with Vlaanderen [Flanders] in 1633. [ASW.182/240]

BOYD, Lord ROBERT, and six servants were permitted to go to France and Flanders for six years in 1583. [NRS.GD8.318]

BOYD, ROBERT, a Captain in Sir Charles Graham's Regiment of Foot in Vlaanderen [Flanders], a deed dated 1696. [NRS.RD4.78.621]

BOYD, THOMAS, the Master of Boyd was permitted to go to France and Flanders for three years, in 1583. [NRS.GD8.319]

BOYT, Colonel Sir DAVID, re a payment due in Flanders or Brabant by Charles du Cruy on 26 May 1587. [NRS.GD305.1.161.29]

BOYTER, WILLIAM, master of the Charming Betty of Anstruther arrived in Anstruther in Fife from Duinkerken [Dunkirk] on 13 January 1749. [NRS.E504.3.1]; William Boytar, master of the Charming Betty of Anstruther from 1745 until 1751, and master of the Rose of Anstruther in 1755. [NRS.E504.3.2/3]

BRANSON, JOHN, servant to John Sleich a merchant in Haddington, East Lothian, aboard ship in Leith, a recruit for the army in Vlaanderen [Flanders], to be put ashore and imprisoned in Canongait Tolbooth, by order of the Privy Council in 1691. [RPCS.XVI.1.127]

BREADSHAW, SAMUEL, a soldier of Lieutenant Colonel Sir Andrew Agnew's Company of the Scots Brigade, [De Schotse Brigade], in Brugge [Bruges] on 13 June 1745. [NRS.GD154.636]

BRENTON, THOMAS, a goldsmith from Clydesdale in Lanarkshire, married Leonora Janszon from Antwerpen [Antwerp] in Rotterdam on 9 September 1590. [Rotterdam Marriage Register]

BRIOCH, JAMES, a shipmaster of Dundee, when bound for Norway, was captured by a French privateer in September 1689, and he and the ship were held in Dunkirk until a ransom of 600 guilders was paid. [LT.581]

BRISBANE, J., a letter stating that the Governor of Oostende [Ostend] had gone to Brogge [Bruges] and reporting on the garrison at Oostende, dated 27 February 1678. [NRAS.165.5.66.388]

BISCHOP, GABRIEL, a Flemish cloth manufacturer, settled in Edinburgh in 1601. [SFP]

BROCKHURST, ARNOLD or ARTHUR, born around 1565, a prospector for gold in Scotland, then a portrait painter in Scotland until 1583, later in London. [PS.31]

BRODIE, ALEXANDER, of Brodie, aboard the Elizabeth of Kirkcaldy at Briel in 1649, a letter for the Conservator of the Scots Privileges. [JTC.191]

BRODIE, DAVID, master of the Mary of Peterhead in Aberdeenshire, from Dunkirk to Leith in 1742; was bound from Leith with a cargo of coal to Dunkirk on 6 July 1743. [NRS.E504.22.1]; from Peterhead to Dunkirk in September 1751. [AJ]

BRODIE, GEORGE, a merchant in Leith, trading with Flanders from 1819 until 1821. [NRS.CS96.3595]

BRODIE, JOHN, master of the Mary of Peterhead in Aberdeenshire from Aberdeen to Duinkerken [Dunkirk] in September 1751. [NRS.E504.1.4] [AJ]

BROG, Sir WILLIAM, Colonel of a Scottish regiment in Vlaanderen [Flanders], a sasine dated 1622. [NRS.RS31.IV.266]

BROWN, ANDREW, master of the James of Kincardine from Anstruther in Fife to Ostende in May 1744. [NRS.E504.3.1]

BROWN, DAVID, a Scot, was married in Bergen op Zoom, Brabant, on 6 September 1719. [WBA]

BROWN, JAMES, a timberman [carpenter] and mariner in Leith, was aboard the John of Leith bound from Vlaanderen [Flanders] to Leith in September 1633. [SJC.I.206]

BROWN, JAMES, married Agnes Mitchell in Namur on 9 September 1719, parents of James Brown who was baptised in Ypren [Ypres] on 19 August 1736. [SB]

BROWN, JAMES, master of the James of Kincardine from Anstruther in Fife to Oostende [Ostend] in May 1745. [NRS.E504.3.1]

BROWN, JAMES, master of the Margaret of Perth trading from Perth to Duinkerken [Dunkirk] in 1767. [NRS.E504.27.4]

BROWN, JAMES, born 1838, son of Thomas Brown and his wife Margaret Balfour in Cellardyke in Fife, died in Antwerpen [Antwerp] on 9 December 1889. [Anstruther Easter gravestone, Fife]

BROWN, JOHN, master of the Charity of Leith, was imprisoned in Oostende [Ostend] in 1632. [XEBR.15.5.1632]

BROUN, JOHN, master of the .....of Leith, with a cargo of plaiding, skins, hides, etc, when bound for Veere was captured by Dunkirkers or residents of West Flanders and was taken to Oostende, Vlaanderen, in March 1632. [RPCS.IV.452]

BROWNE, J., in Antwerpen [Antwerp], a letter to John Drummond, dated 1739. [NRS.GD24.3.389]

BROWN, WILLIAM, in Flanders, agent for George Suttie, a merchant burgess of Edinburgh in 1638. [NRS.GD6.1951]

BROWN, WILLIAM, master of the Katherine of Prestonpans from Prestonpans in Midlothian to Duinkerken [Dunkirk] in1682. [NRS.E72.21.4]

BROWN, WILLIAM, a British Army chaplain in Vlaanderen [Flanders], minister of the Scots Kirk in Utrecht from 1748 until 1757, returned to Scotland. [F.5.555]

BRUCE, JAMES, master of the Alexander of Elie, from Elie in Fife with a cargo of herring bound for Ostend [Oostende], Vlaanderen, in 1711. [NRS.AC8.127]

BRUCE, JOHN, in Antwerpen [Antwerp] a letter dated 1683. [NRS.GD29.2192]

BRUCE, JOHN, of Balcaskie the younger, letters from Brussels and Antwerpen [Antwerp] between 1681 and 1683. [NRS.GD29.1914/2192]

BRUCE, Captain ROBERT, of Woodside, was killed in Vlaanderen [Flanders] in 1677. [SHS.I.469]

BRUCE, Lieutenant ROBERT, of Kennet, at Cambrai, a letter dated 19 June 1817. [NRS.GD124.15.1754]

BRUCE, THOMAS, Earl of Elgin, in Brussels, a letter to Henry Dundas dated 1 January 1793 concerning M. Malonet representative of the planters in St Domingo. [NRS.GD51.1.480]

BRUCE, THOMAS, 7th Earl of Kincardine, a letter to his son William Bruce dated Brussels on 23 March 1716. [NRS.GD160.549]

BRUCE, WILLIAM, a mariner aboard the George of Leith, was imprisoned in Duinkerken [Dunkirk] in 1689. [XEBR.6.11.1689]

BRUCE, WILLIAM, an Ensign of Colonel George Lauder's Regiment of Foot, died in Breda, Flanders, probate 1700, Prerogative Court of Canterbury. [TNA]

BRUCE, WILLIAM, a Sergeant of Captain Lockhart's Company of the Scots Brigade, [De Schotse Brigade], married Kirstin Lamsay, in Terheijden [Terhyde] on 5 July 1746. [SB]

BRYSSON, ABRAHAM, from Lyle in West Flanders, was admitted as a burgess of Edinburgh on 23 July 1633. [EBR]

BRISON, JAMES, from Perth, redeemed 'the bell' in Flanders before 1502. [PKA. Perth Guildry Records]

BUCHAN, GILBERT, from Scotland, married Judith Conjer from Mechelen [Malines] in Leiden on 9 March 1605. [Leiden Marriage Register]

BUCHAN, Colonel, his Regiment of Foot was bound for Flanders in April 1694, vouchers. [NRS.E94.14]

BUCHANAN and SIMPSON, tobacco merchants in Glasgow, trading with Oostende, [Ostend], and Duinkerken [Dunkirk] a letter book from 1759 to 1761. [NRS.CS96.504/7]

BURD, EDWARD, skipper aboard the George of Leith, was imprisoned in Duinkerken [Dunkirk] in 1689. [XEBR.6.11.1689]

BURMEISTER and VAN ZEILER, versus David Buchan in 1810. [NRS.CS271.4784]

BURRAL, JOHN, married Margreit Pell in Yperen [Ypres] on 17 March 1737, parents of Daniela Johanna Burral, who was baptised in Namur on 12 May 1739, also

Cornelia Johanna Burral who was baptised in Charleroi on 2 September 1743. [SB]

BUTCHART, JAMES, master of the George of Montrose, to Duinkerken [Dunkirk] in 1682, 1684, 1685. [NRS.E72.16]; master of the Elizabeth of Dundee bound for Duinkerken [Dunkirk] in 1685. [NRS.E72.7.15]

CAIRNS, DAVID, master of the Joseph of Leith from Duinkerke [Dunkirk] to Leith in September 1681. [NRS.E72.15 23]

CALDWELL, WILLIAM, a Sergeant of Colonel Buchan's Regiment in Vlaanderen [Flanders], deceased by 1696, his widow Janet Hannay and their children settled in Ayr. [NRS.CH2.751.8/135]

CALDWELL, ..., arrived in Scotland from Flanders in 1504. [ATS]

CALLENDAR, WILLIAM, son of Ludovic Callendar of Dorritur, a soldier in Vlaanderen [Flanders], a deed dated 1695. [NRS.RD2.78.1170]

CAMERON, DUNCAN, a Corporal in Captain McKenna's Company of the Scots Brigade, [De Schotse Brigade], married Maria Trese Manfrie, in Charleroi on 17 August 1744, were parents of Elisabeth who was baptised in Yperen [Ypres] on 31 May 1750. [SB]

CAMERON, Lieutenant Colonel EWAN, [who was killed at the Battle of Waterloo] in Brussels, letters to his son Ewan Cameron of Fassifern in 1815. [NRS.GD1.736.138]

CAMERON, JOHN, son of Sir Ewan Cameron of Lochiel and his wife Isabel MacLean, a Jacobite in 1715, who escaped to France and died in Vlaanderen [Flanders] in 1748. [JP.77]

CAMERON, JOHN, son of Donald Cameron, a soldier, and his wife Catherine Fraser, was baptised at Briellel on 20 August 1753. [SB]

CAMPBELL, Captain ALEXANDER, of Fonab, an officer of Argyll's Regiment in Vlaanderen [Flanders] before1694, in the service of the Darien Company in Panama, from 1698 until1699, testament 1739, Comm. Edinburgh. [NRS]

CAMPBELL, ALEXANDER, of Lochdochart, an Ensign of Webb's Regiment in Gent, [Ghent], a letter dated 6 December 1706. [NRS.GD112.39.203.2]

CAMPBELL, Lieutenant ALEXANDER, in Ousterhout, Vlaanderen [Flanders], in 1747. [NRS.GD170.1464A]

CAMPBELL, ANNABELLA, a nun in Antwerpen [Antwerp] sister of the Marquis of Argyll, in 1640s. [NRS.GD40.15.58]

CAMPBELL, ARCHIBALD, 7th Earl of Argyll, in Brussels, letters to his cousin Sir Duncan Campbell, the laird of Glen Orchy, on 16 September 1622, and another dated 31 May 1627. [NRS.GD112.39.5/32.19]

CAMPBELL, ARTHUR, [Aert Cammel], a Scottish soldier under Captain Balfour, married Barbara Veylons from Antwerpen [Antwerp], in Leiden on 25 August 1601. [Leiden Marriage Register]

CAMPBELL, CHRISTINE, letters from Gand [Ghent] dated between1826 and 1832. [NRS.GD113.5.86B]

CAMPBELL, COLIN, Earl of Argyll, was sent on Royal business to France, Flanders and Germany in February 1584. [RPSS.VIII.1855]

CAMPBELL, COLIN, son of Reverend Patrick Campbell in Kenmore, Perthshire, a soldier, probably who had fought in Vlaanderen [Flanders], enlisted as a soldier of the Scots Darien Company, died in Jamaica in 1699, a testament confirmed with the Commissariat of Edinburgh in 1707. [NRS]

CAMPBELL, DONALD, in Brussels, a letter dated 2 April 1842. [NRS.GD170.3238]

CAMPBELL, DOUGALL, a Scot, was married in Bergen op Zoom, Brabant, on 21 June 1719. [WBA]

CAMPBELL, DUNCAN, a mariner aboard the George of Leith, was imprisoned in Duinkerken [Dunkirk] in 1689. [XEBR.6.11.1689]

CAMPBELL, DUNCAN, formerly an Ensign of the Earl of Argyll's Regiment in Vlaanderen [Flanders], later in the Service of the Company of Scotland trading to Africa and the Indies, died in Darien, Panama, in 1699, testament confirmed with the Commissariat of Edinburgh in 1707. [NRS]

CAMPBELL, ELIZABETH, daughter of Malcolm Campbell, a soldier of Major Buchanan's Company, and his wife Christine Cruickshanks, was baptised in Yperen [Ypres] on 17 December 1753 and their son John Campbell was baptised there in March 1754. [SB]

CAMPBELL, FINDLAY, a soldier of Lieutenant Colonel Sir Andrew Agnew's Company of the Scots Brigade, [De Schotse Brigade], in Brugge [Bruges] on 13 June 1745. [NRS.GD154.636]

CAMPBELL, JOHN, of Lundy, the Scottish Ambassador in Flanders in 1540. [RPSS.2.3666]

CAMPBELL, JOHN, a Scottish soldier in Spanish Service in Antwerpen [Antwerp] in 1588, husband of Margaret Burnet. [NRS.GD1.382.959]

CAMPBELL, WILLIAM, [Willem Cammel], a soldier who married Lijntgen Plattevoets, from Poperinge in Vlaalderen [Flanders] in Leiden on 21 November 1604. [Leiden Marriage Register]

CAMPBELL, WILLIAM, a soldier, probably who fought in Vlaanderen [Flanders], died in Darien, Panama, in 1699, testament confirmed with the Commissariat of Edinburgh in 1707. [NRS]

CAMPBELL......, of Glenorchy, in Antwerpen, [Antwerp], a letter dated 1693. [NRS.GD112.163.5]

CANT, WILLIAM, a mariner aboard the George of Leith, was imprisoned in Duinkerken [Dunkirk] in 1689. [XEBR.6.11.1689]

CANZART, COLYN, formerly a resident of Flanders, was permitted to settle in Scotland on 20 February 1510. [RPSS.I.2009]

CARD, JOHN, a soldier of Lieutenant Colonel Sir Andrew Agnew's Company of the Scots Brigade, [De Schotse Brigade], in Brugge [Bruges] on 13 June 1745. [NRS.GD154.636]

CARDONNEL, ADAM, in Gent, [Ghent], a letter dated 19 November 1710. [NRS.GD248.18.4]

CAREU, PETER, master of a Dunkirk privateer, captured the John of Aberdeen, master George Aikman, which was taken to Dunkirk in 1651. [JT.241]

CARKETTLE, JOHN, a Scottish factor, died in Brugge [Bruges] in February 1494. [PL.55]

CARNES, JOHN, a soldier of Captain McGaffray's Company of the Scots Brigade, [De Schotse Brigade], married Mary Jen Barrier, in Yperen [Ypres] on 25 July 1749. [SB]

CARRISON, JOHN, master of the St Albert van Brugge [St Albert of Bruges] from Wemyss in Fife to Brugge with salt on 10 June 1667. [NRS.E29.9]

CASKIE, EILEN, daughter of William Caskie, a soldier of Captain Boyd's Company of the Scots Brigade, [De Schotse Brigade], and his wife Elkie Sauchood, was baptised in Bergen [Mons] in December 1713. [SB]

CASKIE, STEPHEN, son of William Caskie, a soldier of Captain Boyd's Company of the Scots Brigade, [De Schotse Brigade], and his wife Elkie Sauchood, was baptised in Bergen [Mons] in December 1713. [SB]

CASSLE, RICHARD, from Edinburgh, married Maeijke Ver Gracht from Lauwe by Menen, in Bergen op Zoom on 9 October 1585. [Bergen op Zoom marriage register]

CATHROW, THOMAS, a soldier of Lieutenant Colonel Cunningham's Company of the Scots Brigade, [De Schotse Brigade], married Kathrine Gowdine from Kortrijk [Courtrai] on 13 February 1711. [SB]

CAY, WILLIAM, a shipmaster trading between Vlaanderen [Flanders] and Aberdeen in1651. [ASW.337]

CHAMBERS, ALEXANDER, daughter of Robert Chambers, Surgeon Major of the 3rd Regiment of the Scots Brigade, [De Schotse Brigade], was baptised in Doornik [Tournai] on 7 July 1716. [SB]

CHAMBER, DAVID, a Scot from Flanders to Scotland aboard William Acekman's ship, in July 1570. [CSP.III.390]

CHEVAS, Captain, of the John and Robert of Peterhead in Aberdeenshire, bound from London to Peterhead, was captured by the French and taken to Duinkerken [Dunkirk] in 1781. [SM.44.164]

CHIENE, JOHN, master bound f0r Dunkirk on the Generous Betty from Anstruther in Fife to Dunkirk with a cargo of leather goods in March 1751, [NRS.E504.3.2]

CHEYNE, JOHN, of Arnage, Aberdeenshire, graduated from King's College, Aberdeen then studied at Douai in Vlaanderen [Flanders] in 1566. [King's College, Archives]

CHISHOLM, JAMES, an army surgeon in Vlaanderen [Flanders] a deed dated 1696. [NRS.RD4.79.1319]

CHISHOLM, JOHN, a soldier of Captain Cunningham's Company of the Scots Brigade in November 1743. [SB]

CHRISTIE, GEORGE, a Jesuit, son of Andrew Christie a burgess of Dysart, Fife, to be transported to France or

Flanders on board Michael Thomson's ship from Dysart in March 1596. [EBR]

CHRISTIE, JOHN, brother of George Christie the Jesuit, son of Andrew Christie a burgess of Dysart, Fife, in prison, to be banished to France or Flanders on board Michael Thomson's ship from Dysart in March 1596. [EBR]

CLARK, GEORGE, a soldier of Lieutenant Colonel Sir Andrew Agnew's Company of the Scots Brigade, [De Schotse Brigade], in Brugge [Bruges] on 13 June 1745. [NRS.GD154.636]

CLARK, JOHN, in Antwerpen [Antwerp], accounts 1676-1677, reference to Guillaum Boels, a merchant in Antwerpen. [NRS.GD18.2567]

CLARK, JOHN, a soldier of Captain Johnston's Company of the Scots Brigade, [De Schotse Brigade], married Margaret Cattenach, a widow, in Doornik [Tournai] on 2 July 1755. [SB]

CLAUS, ..., a Flemish mariner, aboard John Pendreich's pink, was accused of damage to the ship, in 1558. [ACB.61]

CLAY, IGNATIOUS, in Antwerpen [Antwerp], a letter to Alexander Brand, a merchant in Edinburgh, dated 16 January 1686. [NRS.RH15.53.25]

CLELAND, or HENDERSON, Mrs M., in Brussels, an inventory, 1876. [NRS.181.21]

CLERK, Sir JOHN, of Penicuik, Midlothian, in Brussels, Bergen [Mons], Doornik [Cambrai], and Antwerpen [Antwerp] in 1699. [Memoirs of Sir John Clerk, 1676-1755, Edinburgh, 1892]

CLYNK, ROBERT, a wright, was admitted as a burgess and guilds-brother of Perth on 6 September 1582. [PKA]

CLYNK, WILLIAM, a maltman, was admitted as a burgess and guilds-brother of Perth on 4 September 1583. [PKA]

COCKBURN, JAMES, master of the Peter of Cockenzie, 160 tons, in East Lothian was captured at sea by a French privateer then taken to Oostende [Ostend] where he was imprisoned, in 1677. [NRS.AC7.5]; according to the Register of the Privy Council of Scotland, the ship was bound from Scotland bound for La Rochelle in France but put into Ostend reluctant to go further without a 'pass' which would provide protection from the privateers of Dunkirk, a petition dated May 1677. [RPCS.V.162]

COCKBURN, THOMAS, a shipmaster trading between Niewpoort in Flanders and Riga, Latvia, in 1574. [RAK/STR]

COLE, ANTHONY, born 1616, a mariner in Dunkirk, master of the Angel Keeper of Waterford in 1648, a privateer. [TNA.HCA.15.2.300/820]

COLQUHOUN, Captain JAMES, at Saventhem camp between Brussels and Louvain, a letter dated 18 July 1745. [NRS.GD248.168.6]

COLQUHOUN and RITCHIE, tobacco merchants in Glasgow, trading with Oostende [Ostend] and Duinkerken [Dunkirk] between 1791 and 1809. [NRS.CS96.3994]

CONNICK, WILLIAM, Captain of MacElligott's Regiment in Flanders 1688 until 1689. [IS]

CONTALES, ROBERT, in Ostend, agent for George Macartney, a merchant in Belfast, in 1679. [BMF.142] [LHL.Macartney.2.53/218]

COOK, GEORGE, master of the Rood Leeuw van Oostende [Red Lion of Ostend], arrived in Leith from Vlaanderen [Flanders] in 1666 with a cargo of madder, iron-pots, wire, confectionary, lint seed, grey paper, candy, currants, sugar, starch, hards, shiffon, knitting, silk, Hollands, thimbles, thread and paper. [NRS.E72.15.2]

COOK, JAMES, master of the James arrived in Leith from Oostende [Ostend] with a cargo of tow, soap, hemp and lint in May 1666. [NRS.E72.15.2]

COPLAND, ALEXANDER, son of Lucas Copland, a drummer of Colonel Murray's Company of the Scots Brigade, [De Schotse Brigade], and Rebecca, his wife, was baptised in Doornik [Tournai] on 2 February 1716. [SB]

COPLAND, CHARLES, from Aberdeen, a cooper in Ostend in 1790. [NRS.S/H]

CORNELIUS, BARNARD, a Flemish skipper, master of the Rose from Flanders with a cargo of onions trading with Dundee in 1616. [DSL] [WCB]

CORNELIUS, JANET, daughter of Jan Cornelius a silk weaver and his wife Katherine McClure, was baptised in the Canongait, Edinburgh, on 16 May 1648, later their son John was baptised there. [Canongait parish records]

CORNELISON, JACOB, master of the Dolfijn van Brugge [Dolphin of Bruges], arrived in Leith from Oostende [Ostend] with a cargo of flour, iron, hops, and shiffon in March 1666. [NRS.E72.15.2]

CORNELLIUSON [?], JOHN, [Jan Cornelisz.] a beggar from Scotland, was sent to the galleys for three years and banished from Holland and West Flanders in 1608. [Leiden Court Records .6/136]

CORNTON, GEORGE, and the Royal Treasurer in Flanders in 1508. [ATS]

CORRIE, JOHN, a soldier of the Scots Brigade, [De Schotse Brigade], married Agnes McJeniven, in Yperen [Ypres] on 6 May 1749. [SB]

CORSAR, PETER, master of the Providence of Dundee from Dundee to Duinkerken [Dunkirk] in July 1684. [NRS.E72.7.13]

COTIS, Sir JAMES, was sent to Flanders on the King's business in 1507, and returned with hens etc. [ATS]

COUPAR, ALEXANDER, son of Alexander Coupar, a soldier of Major Alexander's Company of the Scots Brigade, [De Schotse Brigade], and Barbara Dickson, his wife, was baptised in Yperen [Ypres] on 12 July 1734. [SB]

COUPAR, BARBARA, daughter of Alexander Coupar, a soldier of Major Alexander's Company of the Scots Brigade, [De Schotse Brigade], and Barbara Dickson, his wife, was baptised in Doornik [Tournai] on 26 September 1715. [SB]

COUPAR, JOHN, son of Alexander Coupar, a soldier of Major Alexander's Company of the Scots Brigade, [De Schotse Brigade], and Barbara Dickson, his wife, was baptised in Yperen [Ypres] on 17 September 1736. [SB]

COUSTOUN, THOMAS, master of the Grace of God arrived in Dundee from Vlaanderen [Flanders] in December 1638. [DSL]

COUTEAUX, JOHN, master of the St Anna van Brugge [Bruges], from Wemyss in Fife bound for Bruges [Brugge] in July 1667, with a cargo of coal. [NRS.E72.29.9]

COWIE, JEREMY, master of the Peter of Fraserburgh in Aberdeenshire, trading between Vlaanderen [Flanders] and Aberdeen in 1596, and1599. [ASW.25/42]

COX, ALEXANDER, a soldier of Lieutenant Colonel Sir Andrew Agnew's Company of the Scots Brigade, [De Schotse Brigade], in Brugge [Bruges] on 13 June 1745. [NRS.GD154.636]

CRABBE, JOHN, born around 1280, probably in Muiden, Flanders, died around 1352, a privateer who settled as a merchant in Aberdeen after 1310, moved to Berwick in 1318, where he swore allegiance to the King of England, moved to Lincolnshire and died around 1352. [SFP.56]

CRABB, JOHN, was admitted as a burgess and guildsbrother of Perth on 19 September 1488. [PGB][PKA]

CRAIG, DANIEL, a Scot, was married in Bergen op Zoom, Brabant, on 24 December 1758. [SB][WBA]

CRAIG, JOHN, a soldier of the Scots Brigade, [De Schotse Brigade], married Margaret Davis, in Yperen [Ypres] on 22 September 1735. [SB]

CRAIG, JOHN, a Sergeant of Captain Murray's Company of the Scots Brigade, [De Schotse Brigade], married Johanna Halliday in Schaebeek [Scarbek] on 11 September 1745. [SB]

CRANSTON, JAMES, letters from Brugge [Bruges] and Utrecht between 1691 and 1693. [NRS.NRAS.859.16]

CRANSTON, JAMES, an account of the Battle of Steinkirk, a letter dated 7 August 1692. [NRS.GD1.479.9]; a Captain of Colonel James Ferguson's Regiment in Vlaanderen [Flanders], a deed dated 1696. [NRS.RD2.79.838]

CRAWFORD, ESTHER, daughter of James Crawford a merchant in Lanark, married John Smith, a drummer in Colonel Bridget's Regiment in Flanders, a Process of Adherence in 1706. [NRS.CC8.6.138]

CRAWFORD, GRANT, in Brussels, a letter in Dutch to Sir Hew Hamilton on 26 April 1739. [NRS.GD16.1112]

CRIE, LAURENCE, a soldier of Lieutenant Colonel Sir Andrew Agnew's Company of the Scots Brigade, [De Schotse Brigade], in Brugge [Bruges] on 13 June 1745. [NRS.GD154.636]

CROMARTY, ALEXANDER, master of the John of Montrose from Dundee to Duinkerken [Dunkirk] in 1681/1682/1684. [NRS.E72.16.12. 14]

CROMBIE, THOMAS, a prisoner in Edinburgh Tolbooth, was released on condition that he went to Flanders or France never to return, on 24 January 1622. [RPCS.XII.637]

CROMDALE, THOMAS, in Bruges, during 1357 as clerk to the Earl of Mar involved in the ransom payments for King David 11. [David II, East Linton, 2004]

CROOKS, JAMES, from Garnturk, a soldier, probably who fought in Vlaanderen [Flanders], died in Darien, Panama, in 1699, testament confirmed with the Commissariat of Edinburgh in 1707. [NRS]

CRUICKSHANK, ALEXANDER, and six other merchants in Aberdeen, were accused of bringing counterfeit coins from Mechelin [Malines] in 1567. [Accounts of the Treasurer of Scotland, Volume XII.28]

CUMING, ALLEN, a soldier of Major Cameron's Company of the Scots Brigade [De Schotse Brigade], married Elizabeth Van De Putt, a tailor from Kortrijk [Courtrai], in Yperen [Ypres] on 20 November 1716. [SB]

CUMMING, GEORGE, a servant to Sir Patrick Drummond the Conservator of the Scottish Privileges in Belgium, was admitted as a burgess of Aberdeen on 12 May 1641. [ABR]

CUMMING, JAMES, a merchant in Antwerpen [Antwerp] around 1493. [PL.54]

CUMMING, JAMES, a merchant in Breda, Brabant, a sasine, 1772. [NRS.RS27.196.36]

CUNNINGHAM, ADAM, was imprisoned in Oostende [Ostend] by the Spanish, brother of Sir John Cunningham of Labroughtoun, papers from 1677 to 1678. [NRS.GD149.332]

CUNNINGHAM, JOHN, a soldier near Brussels in 1693. [NRS.GD26.13.424]

CUNNINGHAM, ROBERT, a Scottish sugar planter on St Kitts, son of Richard Cunningham of Glenarnock in Ayrshire, trading with Oostende, [Ostend] and Brussels, see ledger from 1715 until 1737. [NRS.CS96.3096/1]

CUNNINGHAM, THOMAS, a Scottish merchant, resident in Veere, a widower, married Josijntgen De Nogelen from Nieupoort in Vlaanderen [Flanders], in Leiden on 19 September 1603. [Leiden Marriage Register]

CUNNINGHAM, Colonel, and his Regiment of Dragoons was bound for Flanders in May 1694, vouchers for pay and subsistence. [NRS.E94.11][25]

CURRAN, SERFF, master of the Hoop van Brugge, [Hope of Bruges], arrived in Bo'ness from Vlaanderen [Flanders] with a cargo of lint-seed, sugar, candy, whalebone, thread, knitting, pots, pans, fustick, wire, and cremerie in January 1667. [NRS.E2.5-]

CURRIE, CHARLES, son of John Currie, a soldier in Captain Irons Company of the Scots Brigade, [De Schotse Brigade], and his wife Agnes McNiven, was baptised in Yperen [Ypres] on 20 April 1749. [SB]

CURRIER, THOMAS, master of the Isobel of Kirkcaldy trading between Oostende [Ostend] and Kirkcaldy in 1666, also between Brugge [Bruges] and Kirkcaldy in Fife with a cargo of cloth, hards and lint on 25 November 1669. [NRS.NRS.E70.9.1/4; E29.9]

DAALHUYSE, KLAAS, master of the Renzee van Oostende trading between Oostende [Ostend] and Dundee in 1782. [NRS.E504.11.10]

DAINDE, JACOB, master of the Keyar arrived in Leith from Brugge [Bruges] with a cargo of lint-seed, brandy, soap, tow, iron, wire, Hollands, knitting, needles, hair-shirts, thread, sugar, nutmeg, mace, silk, aniseed, worsted, lace, cotton ribbons and drugs, in 1666. [NRS.E72.15.2]

DALRYMPLE, Captain HUGH, with the army in Vlaanderen [Flanders] from 1744 until 1745, eight letters. [NRS.GD110.966]

DALRYMPLE, ROBERT, a soldier, letters from Oostende [Ostend] and Gent [Ghent] dated between 1749 and 1756. [NRS.GD110.953]

DALZELL, JOHN, in Ostende, a letter dated 1696. [NRS.GD30.2003]

DAMANE, Sir ADRIAN, of Bisterfield, the Commissioner for Vlaanderen [Flanders] testament confirmed with the Commissariat of Edinburgh on 25 November 1609. [NRS]

DAMANE, FREDERICK, son of Sir Adrian Damane the Commissioner for Vlaanderen [Flanders] testament confirmed with the Commissariat of Edinburgh on 15 June 1610. [NRS]

DAMANE, HADRIAN, son of Sir Adrian Damane the Commissioner for Vlaanderen [Flanders] testament confirmed with the Commissariat of Edinburgh on 15 June 1610. [NRS]

DAMANE, SOPHIA, daughter of Sir Adrian Damane the Commissioner for Vlaanderen [Flanders] testament confirmed with the Commissariat of Edinburgh on 15 June 1610. [NRS]

DANIEL, ROBERT, the British resident in Brussels, six letters to the Earl of Marchmont in 1725. [NRS.GD158.2478]

D'ASSEVILLE, NICHOLAAS, from St Quintin, a cambric weaver, was encouraged to settle in Scotland with ten experienced cambric weavers and their families, to teach cambric weaving there, a total of thirty three arrived in 1729, similarly in 1731 a flax dresser from Flanders arrived in Scotland to teach how to raise and dress flax in 1731. ['The Linen Trade', Alexander Warden,]

DAVIDSON, ARNT, a cramer [pedlar] from Aberdeen, was admitted as a burgess of Antwerpen [Antwerp] in 1598. [SAA]

DAVIDSON, PETER, [Pieter Davidtsz.] from Scotland, married Madelena Fernaus from Ramskappelle near Nieuwpoort in Flanders, in Leiden on 7 March 1587. [Leiden Marriage Register]

DAVIDSON, WILLIAM, a burgess of Dundee, returned from Vlaanderen [Flanders] in 1611. [RPCS.IX.260]

DAVIS, JEAN, daughter of Richard Davis a Corporal in Captain Watson's Company of the Scots Brigade, [De Schotse Brigade], was baptised in Yperen [Ypres] on 4 December 1750. [SB]

DAVIS, MARGRITA JOANNA, daughter of Richard Davis a Corporal in Captain Watson's Company of the Scots Brigade, [De Schotse Brigade], was baptised in Yperen [Ypres] on 27 December 1736. [SB]

EUSTACE, ALAN, a merchant in Perth by 2 November 1459. [PGR.60]

DAW, ANDREW, master of the Patience of Montrose Angus, arrived in Dundee from Duinkerken [Dunkirk] in March 1681. [NRS.E72.16.2]

DE BETHUNE, ROBERT, a witness to a De Quincy charter between 1165 AD and 1190 AD. [KS.319]

DE CARVIN, ROBERT, witnessed a document around 1170 AD. [NRS.GD241.254][KS.319]

DE CORTHY, Sir ANSELM ASOUNES, and his son Anselm, merchants from Brugge [Bruges] were admitted as burgesses and guild-brothers of Perth on 14 February 1682. [PGB]

DE COURRIERES, ALAN, a witness at Newbattle Abbey in Midlothian, in 1170. [KS.319][SHR.XXX.45]

DE FOBIANA, Compte E., in Brussels, a letter to Ewan Cameron of Fassifan, dated 1815. [NRS.GD1.736.143]

DE LA RUDGE, JACQUIS, a camber and a spinner, settled in Perth around 1601. [SFP]

DE LENS, HUGH, settled in Scotland around 1100. [SFP]

DE LETTRE, JEAN BAPTISTE master of Notre Dame de Dunkerque, arrived in Greenock from Dunkerque, [Dunkirk], on 8 October 1742. [NRS.E504.1]

DE DAMPIERRE, MARGARET, daughter of Guy de Dampierre, alias Gwijde van Dampiere, the Count of Flanders, married Alexander, [1264 – 1284], son of

Alexander II King of Scotland, in Roxburgh, Scotland, on 11 November 1292. [SFP]

DE FRISCOBALD, a Lombard merchant, and his factor Johan, purchased textiles in Flanders which were sent to King James IV of Scotland, 2 May 1505. [ATS]; he sent a cloth of gold, satin, taffeta, and silver tableware to the Queen of Scotland in 1507. [ATS]

DE LA COURT, ABRAHAM, overseer of the manufactury in Ayr, a bond, dated 25 June 1663. [NRS.RD4.7.930]

DE MANCELL, CHARLES, in Strathmiglo, Fife, a translation and an assignment, 1 August 1664. [NRS.RD4.11.320/327]

DE ORCHIA, ROGER, settled in Scotland in the 12th century. [SFP]

DE QUINCY, ROBERT, from Cuinchy in French Flanders, settled in Leuchars, Fife, in the 12th century. [SFP]

DERICKSON, JAN, master of the Joseph van Brugge, [Joseph of Bruges] arrived in Bo'ness, West Lothian, with a cargo of deals and trees in June 1667. [NRS.E72.5.]

DERMIS, CORNELIUS, a Flemish weaver, settled in Dundee in 1601. [SFP.66]

DE RUDER, PETER, master of a Dunkirk privateer, captured the John of Aberdeen, master George Aikman, which was taken to Dunkirk in 1651. [JT.241]

DE MALLANDER, FRANCIS, a merchant in Bruges, [Brugge] versus George Clark a merchant in Edinburgh in 1686. [NRS.HCAS]

DE SCHODT, ALEXANDER, a merchant in Antwerpen, [Antwerp] freighted the St Francis van Antwerpen to sail from Oostende [Ostend] via Dublin bound for Scotland, which was shipwrecked near Portpatrick in Scotland in 1666. [NRS.RH9.5.31]

DE TURK, HENRI, a Flemish cloth maker, settled, via Norwich, England, in Dundee around 1601. [SFP.66]

DE VOS, JAN, a harpooner aboard the Peggy of Glasgow arrived in Bo'ness, West Lothian, on 1 October 1751, from Greenland. [NRS.E508.48.8]

DE VOOS, JAN, master of the Sint Jan van Duinkirken [St John of Dunkirk], a captured privateer, was condemned by the High Court of the Admiralty of Scotland on 12 August 1711. [NRS.AC7.9.196]

DE VOOYLAR, JAN, master of the Phoenix van Brugge, from Bo'ness in West Lothian with a cargo of coal bound for Vlaanderen [Flanders] in October 1666. [NRS.E72.5-]

DE WILDE, Captain, plans of his house in Antwerpen [Antwerp] in 1729. [NRS.RHP.13257/17]

DICK,........, master of the William of Airth in Stirlingshire, from Aberdeen bound for Duinkerken [Dunkirk] in October 1751. [AJ.199]

DICKSON, ALEXANDER, a Scot, was married in Bergen op Zoom on 14 December 1636. [WBA]

DICKSON, ALEXANDER, a Lieutenant of De Offerell's Regiment in Vlaanderen [Flanders], petitioned the Privy Council for recruits, in 1691. [RPCS.XVI.1.67]

DICKSON, DAVID, from Errol in Perthshire, a wool-comber in Leiden, married Marytgen Kaene from Kortrijk [Courtrai], Flanders, in Leiden on 12 October 1596; was admitted as a burgess of Leiden on 17 October 1608. [Leiden Marriage Register] [Leiden Citizenship Book]

DICKSON, JANET, daughter of John Dickson a soldier of Captain Irons Company of the Scots Brigade, [De Schotse Brigade], was baptised in Veuren [Furnes] on 10 August 1734. [SB]

DICKSON, ROBERT, a Flemish silk weaver in Perth, was authorised to teach the skill of silk weaving in 1581. [PKA]

DICKSON, ROBERT, [Robbert Dircxz.] a Scottish seaman living on the Maeslants Huys, widower of Lijsbeth Tomas, married Jannetgen Andries from Menen [in Flanders] in Leiden on 7 September 1614. [Leiden Marriage Register]

DOBIE, ALEXANDER, from Bellie in Moray, a Sergeant of the Gordon Highlanders, was killed at Egmont-op-Zee in 1799. [HGH.27]

DOBIE, RICHARD, was bound for Flanders in May 1599 to recruit masons and workmen to repair the roof of the church in Edinburgh, also to obtain tar. [EBR]

DODS, ANNA MARIE, daughter of Robert Dods, a soldier of Captain Graham's Company of the Scots Brigade, [De Schotse Brigade] and his wife Johanna, was baptised in Veurne [Ffurne] on 13 January 1750. [SB]

DON, JAMES, a soldier of Captain Orrock's Company of the Scots Brigade, [De Schotse Brigade], married Margret Peterson, in Keerbergen on 4 May 1746. [SB]

DON, JOHN, a Scot, was married in Bergen op Zoom on 14 April 1734. [WBA]

DON, THOMAS, a Corporal of Colonel Gordon's Company in the Scots Brigade, [De Schotse Brigade], married Margaret Carr, in Doornik [Courtrai] on 14 August 1770. [SB]

DOUGALL, THOMAS, a Scot, was married in Bergen op Zoom on 17 December 1718. [WBA]

DOUGLAS, GEORGE, an Ensign, probably who fought in Vlaanderen [Flanders], died in Darien, Panama, testament confirmed with the Commissariat of Edinburgh in 1707. [NRS]

DOUGLAS, JAMES, born 1612, a soldier, was granted a pass to travel to Bergen op Zoom, Brabant, on 31 August 1635. [TNA.E157.20]

DOUGLAS, JAMES, born 1617, son of William Douglas the Earl of Angus, Colonel of a Scottish Regiment, formerly commanded by Sir John Hepburn, was killed at Douai, Vlaanderen, [Flanders], on 21 October 1645. [SP.I.204]

DOUGLAS, Sir JAMES, born 1671, Colonel of the Cameronian Regiment, was killed at the Battle of Steenkerken [Steinkirk] on 3 August 1692.

DOUGLAS, JOHN, the Earl of Angus, son of James, the 2nd Marquis of Douglas, was killed at the Battle of Steinkirk in 1692. [NRS.CH1.5.172]

DOUGLAS, PETER, a Captain of a Scottish Company in Vlaanderen, [Flanders], a testament confirmed with the Commissariat of Edinburgh on 12 February 1583, [NRS]

DOUGLAS, PHILIP, a soldier who was granted a pass to travel to Vlaanderen [Flanders] on 26 May 1631. [TNA.E157.15]

DOUGLAS, ROBERT, master of the Anna of Leith from Leith to Vlaanderen [Flanders] in August 1681. [NRS.E72.15.24]

DOUGLAS, ROBERT, of Glenbervie, was Colonel of the Scots Greys at the Battle of Steinkirk in Vlaanderen [Flanders] in 1692.

DOUGLAS, ROBERT, from Edinburgh, was in Bergen op Zoom on 26 June 1754. [WBA]

DOUGLAS, WILLIAM, a soldier who was granted a pass to travel to Vlaanderen [Flanders] on 11 August 1635. [TNA.E157.20]

DOW, JOHN, a Scot, was married in Bergen op Zoom, on 23 March 1707. [WBA]

DOWNIE, JAMES, master of the Interest of Leith, with a cargo of salt bound for Middleburg in Zealand, was captured by a privateer based in Duinkerken [Dunkirk] in 1630, a case before the High Court of the Admiralty of Scotland in 1631. [NRS.AC7]

DROMMEL, HENRY, of Kinkell in Fife, a smith, who married Elizabeth Dobbie from Brugge [Bruges] in Leiden on 3 June 1604. [Leiden Marriage Register]

DRUMMOND, GEORGE, [Joris Drommon], married Hester Doube from Brugge [Bruges] in Leiden on 23 November 1596. [Leiden Marriage Register]

DRUMMOND, JOHN, of Quarrel, a letter from Charles Boyle, the 4th Earl of Orrery in Brussels, dated 21 September 1711. [NRS.GD24.5.72]

DRUMMOND, JOHN, Commissary in Antwerpen [Antwerp] in 1738. [JCTP.47.82]

DRUMMOND, JOHN, received four letters from D. de Dieu in Antwerpen [Antwerp] in 1739. [NRS.GD24.3.394]

DRUMMOND, ROBERT, formerly a Cornet of Lord Jedburgh's Regiment in Flanders, later was Captain of the Caledonia at Darien, Panama, a decreet dated 29 May 1702. [NRS.NRAS.0364.63]

DRUMMOND, THOMAS, master of the Providence of Dundee from Dundee to Oostende [Ostend] in October 1664. [NRS.E72.7.1]

DRUMMOND, THOMAS, from Edinburgh, a soldier, probably who fought in Vlaanderen [Flanders], died in Darien, Panama, testament confirmed with the Commissariat of Edinburgh in 1707. [NRS]

DRUMMOND, WILLIAM, a Scottish tailor, was admitted as a citizen of Antwerpen [Antwerp] in 1537. [SA. Antwerpen, Poorterboek]

DRUMMOND, WILLIAM, Colonel of the Scots Fusilier Guards, a letter from Brussels to his sister Euphemia Drummond, on 2 February 1815. [NRS.GD1.1036]

DRUMMOND, ..., Duke of Perth, was in Bergen op Zoom. Brabant, a letter dated 1711. [NRS.GD16.35.43]

DU MULLANDER, FRANCIS, a merchant in Brugge [Bruges], versus George Clark, a merchant in Edinburgh, re a debt of 4260 guilders, a case before the High Court of the Admiralty of Scotland on 29 June 1686. [NRS.AC7.7]

DUNBAR, THOMAS, was commissioned as an Ensign of Captain Williamson's Company of Handyside's Regiment in Brussels in 1744. [NRS.NRAS.3094.472]

DUNCAN, GABRIEL or GIDEON, in Oostende, [Ostend], eight letters in 1792. [NRS.NRAS.3955.60.1.191/218]

DUNCAN, GEORGE, master of the George of Bo'ness from Alloa, Stirlingshire, with a cargo of coal bound for Ostend [Oostende] in November 1690. [NRS.E72.5.38]

DUNDAS, WALTER, son of Robert Dundas in Harbiston, a soldier, probably who fought in Vlaanderen [Flanders], died in Darien, Panama, testament confirmed with the Commissariat of Edinburgh in 1707. [NRS]

DUNLOP, JAMES, a mariner aboard the George of Leith, was imprisoned in Duinkerken [Dunkirk] in 1689. [XEBR.6.11.1689]

DURIE, GEORGE, a student at Douai College in French Flanders, a letter to his brother Henry Durie in Dunfermline, Fife, formerly at Louvain University, two letters on 1 December 1575. [NRS.GD1.229.2/3]

DURIE, JOHN, a student at Douai College in French Flanders, a letter to his brother Henry Durie in Dunfermline, Fife, formerly at Louvain University, two letters on 1 December 1575. [NRS.GD1.229.2/3]

ECHLIN, HENRY, grandson of Henry Echlin of Pittadro, a soldier in Flanders in 1623. [NRS.GD172.114]

ECKLEY, THOMAS, a soldier of Lieutenant Colonel Sir Andrew Agnew's Company of the Scots Brigade [De Schotse Brigade], in Brugge [Bruges] on 13 June 1745. [NRS.GD154.636]

EDMONSTOUN, GILBERT, was to pay Jerome de Fiscobald in Flanders in 1505. [ATS]

EGBERT, PIETER, master of the Wobbegynna van Oostende trading between Oostende [Ostend] and Dundee in 1783. [NRS.E504.11.11]

ELESERT, PIETER, master of a ketch with cargo from Oostende [Ostend] to Aberdeen in 1665. [ASW.525]

ELLIOT, JOHN, a soldier who was granted a pass to travel to Vlaanderen [Flanders] on 26 May 1631. [TNA.E157.15]

ELMERTS, CORNELIUS, a harpooner aboard the Dundee of Dundee arrived in Dundee in 1754, from Greenland. [NRS.E508.51.8]

ELMERTS, LUNDERT, a harpooner aboard the Dundee of Dundee arrived in Dundee on 25 July 1753, also in 1754, from Greenland. [NRS.E508.51.8]

ERSKINE, HARRY, in Breda, Brabant, a letter in 1702. [NRS.GD124.15.220]

ERSKINE, JAMES, master of the Katherine of Aberdeen from Aberdeen via Montrose in Angus, to Duinkerken [Dunkirk] in August 1749. [NRS.E504.1.3// 24.2]

ERSKINE, THOMAS, son of the deceased Colonel Lues Erskine, appointed Major General Sir Thomas Livingstone as his factor, subscribed in Brussels, Brabant, on 12 November 1693. [NRS.GD305.1.161.29]

ESPLIN, JOHN, a soldier, probably who fought in Vlaanderen [Flanders], enlisted in the Scots Darien Company, was bound from Leith aboard the Unicorn on 14 July 1698, for Darien, Panama, died there on 1 July 1700. [DP.352]

EUSTACE, ALAN, was admitted as a burgess and guildsbrother of Perth on 25 December 1484. [PKA]

EVANS, alias POWELL, Mrs, a servant of Lady Nithsdale, a letter from Sluyis near Oostende [Ostend] dated 28 June 1716. NRS.NRAS.3666.18.1O]

FALCONER, MICHAEL, master of the Fortune arrived in Leith from Niewpoort, Flanders, in 1666 with a cargo of French hops. [NRS.E72.]

FERGUSON, ALEXANDER, from Maybole, Ayrshire, a soldier, probably who fought in Vlaanderen [Flanders], died in Darien, Panama, in 1699, testament confirmed with the Commissariat of Edinburgh in 1707. [NRS]

FERGUSON, GEORGE, a Scot, was married in Bergen op Zoom, on 3 May 1628. [WBA]

FERGUSON, JAMES, a Scot, was married in Bergen op Zoom, on 3 October 1634. [WBA]

FERGUSON, Colonel JAMES, his Regiment of Foot returned from Flanders in April 1699, vouchers; he was bound for Flanders in March 1702. [NRS.E94.63/108]

FERGUSON, JANET, daughter of Duncan Ferguson, a soldier in Colonel Houston's Company of the Scots Brigade, [De Schotse Brigade], was baptised in Yperen [Ypres] on 16 February 1754. [SB]; Janet Ferguson, from Yperen, married Duncan Sharp from Campbeltown, Argyll, in the Scots Kirk in Rotterdam on 12 February 1774. [GAR]

FERGUSON, JOHN, master of the barque Helen of Dunbar in East Lothian, which was captured by a French privateer, the Koningen van Oostende [Queen of Ostend] and the ship's apprentice was imprisoned in Oostende [Ostend] awaiting ransom in 1704. [NRS.AC9.46]

FERGUSON, REBECCA, daughter of John Ferguson a grenadier of Colonel Gordon's Regiment of the Scots Brigade, [De Schotse Brigade], was baptised in Sluis on 27 September 1767. [SB]

FERGUSON, ROBERT, a merchant in Antwerp, ['Handwart'] agent for William Wilson in Dunfermline in Fife for the sale of a cargo of hides in 1449. [Dunfermline Guild Court Book 15 February 1449]

FERMANT, PHILIP, a Flemish weaver, was permitted to settle in Scotland and follow his trade there in 1587.   [SFP.63]

FIDDES, ROBERT, master of the Margaret returned to Aberdeen from Vlaanderen [Flanders] in September 1617; in May 1619; from Aberdeen to Vlaanderen [Flanders] in August 1619. [ASW.89/101]

FINDLATOR, ANDREW, from Aberdeen to Vlaanderen [Flanders] in March 1638. [ASW.232]

FINDLAY, DUFF, and Company, merchants in Glasgow trading with Antwerp from 1826 until 1842. [NRS.CS96.4810]

FINLAY, HANS, a Lieutenant of Colonel John Buchan's Regiment of Foot in Vlaanderen [Flanders], a deed dated 1699. [NRS.RD4.83.771]

FINLAY, PATRICK, from Vlaanderen [Flanders] to Aberdeen in May 1619. [ASW.101]

FLEMING, JOHN, [Jan de Vlaeminck] was a citizen of Antwerpen [Antwerp] around 1540. [SA. Antwerpen, Poorterboek]

FLEMING, PETER, a soldier of Lieutenant Colonel Sir Andrew Agnew's Company of the Scots Brigade, [De Schotse Brigade], in Brugge [Bruges] on 13 June 1745. [NRS.GD154.636]

FLEMING, THOMAS, a merchant burgess of Edinburgh, freighted a cargo of Spanish wine, wheat, salt, etc, from Rotterdam bound for Leith in 1650, in a ship of Rotterdam, master Robert Williamson, which was seized by three frigates under Captain Nicolas Helt, William O'Doran, and Claude Collet and owned by Cornelius Claesson Van De Zip, a case before the King of Spain at a Privy Council in Brussels in August 1650. [JTC.234]

FLEMISMAN, PETER, a mason employed at the construction of Falkland Palace in Fife around 1540. [AMW.1.256]

FLEUCKER, JOHN, a mariner aboard the George of Leith, was imprisoned in Duinkerken [Dunkirk] in 1689. [XEBR.6.11.1689]

FLUTHMAN, THOMAS, from Vlaanderen [Flanders], was admitted as a burgess and guilds-brother of Perth on 19 September 1488. [PGB]

FOGO, JAMES, a privateer, attacked and looted ships of Oostende [Ostend] then sold the cargoes in England, on his return to Scotland King James V ordered his imprisonment in 1540. [The Letters of James V, Edinburgh, 1954]

FORBES, ALEXANDER, a 'fireworker' in the English train of Artillery in Vlaanderen [Flanders] in 1697. [NRS.GD52.110]

FORBES, CHARLES, formerly a Captain of Hill's Regiment in Vlaanderen [Flanders], from Leith aboard the Unicorn bound for Darien, Panama on 14 July 1698, was employed at the Darien colony in 1698-1699, died on the return voyage to Scotland at Matanzas Bay, Cuba, on 25 July 1699. [DD.225][DP.196]

FORBES, JOHN, son of Donald Forbes and his wife Grissel MacDonald, was baptised in Yperen [Ypres] on 7 September 1767. [SB]

FORBES, MARY, daughter of Donald Forbes and his wife Grissel MacDonald, was baptised in Yperen [Ypres] on 14 November 1768. [SB]

FORBES, PETER, an Ensign of Colonel Mackay's Regiment, married Sarah Jacoba Grahame, in Ath on 17 July 1747. [SB]

FORBES, WILLIAM, a soldier from Aberdeen, married Jenneke Heyndricks in Sluis on 2 November 1626. [Sluis Marriage Register]

FORBES, WILLIAM, of Kirky, in Gent [Ghent] around 1740, a letter. [NRS.RH15.1.162]

FORFAR, Earl of, a soldier in Breda, Brabant, a letter dated 8 January 1712. [NRS.NRAS.2177.5306]

FORRET, Sir WILLIAM, a Captain of Lancers in the Service of Flanders, died in 1600. [St Walburgaskerk monumental inscription, Brugge [Bruges].

FORREST, JOHN, master of the Friendship of London from Aberdeen to Duinkerken [Dunkirk] in October 1750. [NRS.E504.1.3]

FORREST, ROBERT, versus Geylen Schott, son of Adrian Scott, the Commander of the Zoon [Sun] from Curacao, a petition before the High Court of the Admiralty of Scotland in 1707. [NRS.AC10.66]

FORRESTER, ROBERT, born 1616, master of the Unicorn arrived in Dundee in October 1639 from Vlaanderen [Flanders]. [DSL]

FORSTER, JOHN, [Jan Forster] a merchant from Leith, was admitted as a burger of Antwerpen [Antwerp] in 1537. [SA.Antwerpen, Pooerterboek]

FOTHERINGHAM, Sir ALEXANDER, a priest, complained that though Scottish skippers, when at Brugge [Bruges], were supposed to pay at the altar of St Ninian in the church of the Carmelites there, most refused to do so. [LJV.83]

FOTHERINGHAM DANIEL, a soldier of Lieutenant Colonel Sir Andrew Agnew's Company of the Scots Brigade, [De Schotse Brigade], in Brugge [Bruges] on 13 June 1745. [NRS.GD154.636]

FOULAR, LAURENS, from Dunfermline, in Fife, was trading in Flanders in 1572. [Dunfermline Court Book, 1433-1597]

FRANK, PETER, a smith in Edinburgh Castle in 1625. [SFP.66]

FRANCESS, PIETER, a Fleming residing in Veere, versus Andrew Maling in Leith, who had arrested his pink, before the Admiralty Court in August 1558. [ACB.69]

FRANCIS, JOHN, was appointed as Conservator of the Scots Privileges in Flanders, Brabant, Zealand and Holland on 31 December 1507; 6 June 1508. He replaced the deceased Andrew Haliburton. [RPSS.I.1583;1687][ATS]

FRASER, ALEXANDER, a soldier, probably who fought in Vlaanderen and [Flanders], died in Darien, Panama, in 1699, testament confirmed with the Commissariat of Edinburgh in 1707. [NRS]

FRASER, ALEXANDER, of Culduthel, former Captain of Lord George Murray's Regiment of Foot, who died in Bergen op Zoom on 27 July 1747, versus Jean Connelly relict of John Petry a soldier, now married to George Reynolds, a soldier of Lieutenant General James Sinclair's Regiment of Foot, who were married in Bruges on 21 November 1744. A Process of Declarator of Marriage, 1752. [NRS.CC8.6.340]

FRASER, CATHERINE, daughter of Lauchlan Fraser, a soldier in Captain Watson's Company of the Scots Brigade, [De Schotse Brigade], was baptised in Yperen [Ypres] on 3 July 1746 [SB]

FRASER, CATHERINE, daughter of Thomas Fraser and his wife Johanna Robertson, was baptised in Yperen [Ypres] on 12 June 1768. [SB]

FRASER, DAVID, son of Lauchlan Fraser a soldier in Captain Watson's Company of the Scots Brigade, [De Schotse Brigade], was baptised in Terhyde on 3 July 1746. [SB]

FRASER, DAVID, son of John Fraser and his wife Margaret Fraser, was baptised in Yperen [Ypres] on 3 July1768. [SB]

FRASER, ELISABETH, daughter of Alexander Fraser, a Sergeant of Major Dundas's Company of the Scots Brigade, [De Schotse Brigade], and his wife Rachel Mill, was baptised in Yperen [Ypres] on 21 January 1754. [SB]

FRASER, ISABEL, daughter of Lauchlan Fraser a soldier i Captain Watson's Company of the Scots Brigade, [De Schotse Brigade], was baptised in Yperen [Ypres] on 24 August 1750. [SB]

FRASER, Lieutenant JOHN, a letter from the battlefield near Bergen [Mons], dated 11 September 1709. [NRS.GD406.1.10340]

FRASER, JOHN, a soldier of Captain MacLean's Company of the Scots Brigade, [De Schotse Brigade], married Margaret McKenzie, in Yperen [Ypres] on 27 February 1732. [SB]

FRASER, KATHERINE, daughter of Alexander Fraser, a Sergeant of Major Dundas's Company of the Scots Brigade, [De Schotse Brigade], and his wife Rachel Mill, was baptised in Yperen on 3 March 1749. [SB]

FRASER, MALCOLM, of Culduthel, Inverness-shire, formerly a Captain of Lord John Murray's Regiment of Foot, died in Bergen op Zoom on 27 July 1747. [NRS.CC8.6.340]

FRASER, THOMAS, a soldier of Captain Mackenzie's Company of the Scots Brigade, [De Schotse Brigade], married Mary Johnston from Glasgow, in Doornik, [Tournai] on 6 May 1720. [SB]

FRASER, WILLIAM, master of the James and John of Dundee from Dundee to Duinkerken [Dunkirk] in September 1681. [NRS.E72.7.8]

FRATER, ARTHUR WELLESLEY, was born on 20 October 1852 in Aberdeen, son of James Frater and his wife Mary Lowe, was educated at Aberdeen University in 1875, later a minister in Middelburg and Flushing in the Netherlands, later in Belgium, from 1884. [F.7.549]

FRESKIN, a Fleming, was granted the lands of Innes and Nether Urquhart in Moray around 1150. [SFP]

FULLERTON, HUGH, a Captain of Colonel Ferguson's Regiment in Vlaanderen [Flanders], a deed dated 1697. [NRS.RD4.80.835]

GALBRAITH, JAMES, the King's panitier [pantryman], purchased six covers from Doornik [Tournai] for the use of King James VI in March 1575. [ATS.XIII.96/192]

GAMEL, DAVID, son of John Gamel, a soldier of Lieutenant Halkett's Company of the Scots Brigade, [De Schotse Brigade], and his wife Margaret Snith, was baptised in Yperen [Ypres] on 23 October 1732. [SB]

GARDEN, JOHN, a Flemish weaver, was permitted to settle in Scotland and follow his trade there in 1587. [SFP.63]

GARDINER, Colonel JAMES, in Gent, [Ghent] letters from 1742 until 1743. [NRS.498.1.16-22]; in Oostende [Ostend], a letter to Lady Frances Gardiner in Edinburgh, dated 28 August 1742. [NRS.GD498.1.15]

GARDYNE, GEORGE, master of the barque Allan of Dundee arrived in Dundee from Vlaanderen [Flanders] in 1614. [DSL]

GARNAUD, MARTIN, master of the Matrimony arrived in Leith from Oostende and Brugge [Ostend and Bruges] in April 1666 with a cargo of iron, madder, wine, paper, soap, whinstone, apothecary ware and tow. [NRS.E72.15.2]

GARRISON, JOHN, master of the St Albert van Brugge [St Albert of Bruges], from Wemyss in Fife bound for Bruges [Brugge] in July 1667, with a cargo of coal. [NRS.92.9]

GATT, JAMES, a mariner aboard the George of Leith, was imprisoned in Duinkerken [Dunkirk] in 1689. [XEBR.6.11.1689]

GAY, DAVID, master of the David arrived in Dundee in July 1638 from Vlaanderen [Flanders]. [DSL]

GAY, WILLIAM, a Captain of Colonel Brudnall's Regiment of Foot in Vlaanderen [Flanders], a deed dated 1696. [NRS.RD4.78.188]

GEDDES, DAVID, in Bergen op Zoom, Brabant, son of Robert Geddes of Scotstoun, a letter dated 17 October 1733. [NRS.RH15.70.26]

GENT, JOHN and WILLIAM, in Perth between 1569 and 1584. [NRS.B59.8.1]

GERARD, GEORGE, born 1790, eldest son of George Gerard of Midstrath, of the 42nd [Black Watch] Regiment, was killed in action at Les Quatre Bras in Flanders on 16 June 1815. [AJ]

GERARD, NICOLAS, in Perth in 1594. [NRS.B59.8.6.39B]

GERBIER, BALTHAZAR, in Brussels a letter to the Marquis of Hamilton concerning the King of Sweden and the wars, dated 24 August 1631. [NRS.GD406.1.208]

GIBB, JOHN, master of the George trading between Flanders and Dundee in 1618. [DSL]

GILBERT, WILLIAM, a Corporal of Lieutenant Colonel Sir Andrew Agnew's Company of the Scots Brigade, [De Schotse Brigade], in Brugge [Bruges] on 13 June 1745. [NRS.GD154.636]

GILCHRIST, WILLIAM, son of William Gilchrist a soldier of Captain Graham's Company of the Scots Brigade, [De Schotse Brigade], was baptised in Yperen [Ypres] on 8 December 1734. [SB]

GILLESPIE, ROBERT, a drummer of Lieutenant Colonel Sir Andrew Agnew's Company of the Scots Brigade, [De Schotse Brigade], in Brugge [Bruges] on 13 June 1745. [NRS.GD154.636]

GILMOUR, GEORGE, to Westen Vlaanderen [West Flanders] to be educated in 1641. [NRS.GD122.2.559]

GLATHERY, THOMAS, a drummer of Lieutenant Colonel Sir Andrew Agnew's Company of the Scots Brigade, [De Schotse Brigade], in Brugge [Bruges] on 13 June 1745. [NRS.GD154.636]

GOLDMAN, CHARLES, a burgess of Dundee, returned there from Vlaanderen [Flanders] in 1611. [RPCS.IX.260]

GORDON, ALEXANDER, of Kinstair, a Lieutenant of the Earl of Angus's Regiment of Foot in Vlaanderen [Flanders], was admitted as a burgess and guild-brother of Ayr on 1 February 1692. [Ayr Burgess Roll]

GORDON, Sir ALEXANDER, a Lieutenant Colonel, brother of the Earl of Aberdeen, was killed at the Battle of Waterloo, a letter from the Duke of Wellington dated 19 June 1815. [NRAS.555.8.12][NRS.GD274.1031.5]

GORDON, CHARLES, of Kirdells, a Captain of Colonel Lauder's Regiment in Flanders, in 1694. Correspondent in John Grant versus Ann Leslie. [NRS. CC8.6.67]

GORDON, COSMO GEORGE, Duke of Gordon, was in Brussels in 1748. [NRS.GD44.33.30]

GORDON, DONALD, born 1784, a smuggler and horse-trader from Gernside, Aberdeenshire, was accused of forging documents in Kales [Calais] in 1830. [NRS.AD14.30.12]

GORDON, GEORGE, Lieutenant Colonel of the 42nd [Black Watch] Regiment and of the 3rd Guards Regiment, served in Flanders. He became the 5th Duke of Gordon and died in 1836. [HGH.19]

GORDON, JAMES, born 1615, a soldier, was granted a pass to travel to Antwerpen [Antwerp] in 1632. [TNA.E157.16]

GORDON, MARIAH ROBERTINA, daughter of Lieutenant Colonel James Gordon of the Scots Brigade, [De Schotse Brigade], and his wife Dame Johanna Mariah Hyndryck, [Heij den Rijk] was baptised in Yperen [Ypres] on 11 November 1733. [SB]

GORDON, MEMSO, son of Lieutenant Colonel James Gordon of the Scots Brigade, [De Schotse Brigade], and his wife Dame Johanna Mariah Hyndryck, [Heij den Rijk] was baptised in Yperen [Ypres] on18 October 1732.[SB]

GORDON, Captain ROBERT, captured the privateer
Holy Trinity of Ostend, [Oostende], master Jean Sable
in 1705. [NRS.AC9.130]

GORDON, ROBERT, a soldier of Lieutenant Colonel
Cunningham's Company of the Scots Brigade, [De
Schotse Brigade], married Kathrin Porties, daughter
of John Porties in Kortrijk [Tournai] in Yperen [Ypres]
on 3 April 1716. [SB]

GORDON, THOMAS, master of the Royal Mary,
captured the Holy Trinity of Ostend a privateer in 1705.
[NRS.HCA.AC7.107]

GORDON, THOMAS, a Scot, was married in Bergen op
Zoom on 13 November 1733. [WBA]

GORDON, WALTER, master of the Good Hope of Aberdeen,
trading from Duinkerken [Dunkirk] to Aberdeen in 1742.
[NRS.E504.1.1]

GORDON, WILLIAM, a Captain in ....'s Regiment
in Vlaanderen [Flanders] a deed dated 1695.
[NRS.RD2.79.9]

GOSBEY, RICHARD, a soldier of Lieutenant Colonel Sir
Andrew Agnew's Company of the Scots Brigade, [De
Schotse Brigade] in Brugge [Bruges] on 13 June 1745.
[NRS.GD154.636]

GOURLAY, JAMES, a Scot, was married in Bergen op
Zoom on 17 August 1649. [WBA]

GOURLAY, JOHN, master of the Hopndeee of Leith
from Leith bound for Vlaanderen [Flanders] in March
1672. [NRS.E72.15.11]

GOURLAY, ROBERT, [Robrecht Gourla] a citizen of
Antwerpen [Antwerp] in 1540.
[SA.Antwerpen.Poorterboek]

GOURLAY, ROBERT, in Leith, a letter to Odenhove,
Buff, and Company in Antwerp in 1830.
[NRS.GD31.4949]

GOUSHANE, CLAUS, a merchant in Oostende
[Ostend] trading with Leith in 1665. [NRS.E72.15.2]

GRAHAM, DAVID, of Fintry, was permitted on 14 December 1588 to go via Dundee to France and Flanders and remain there until King James IV authorised his return. [RPCS.IV.337]

GRAHAM, DONALD, a Corporal of Captain Murray's Company of the Scots Brigade, [De Schotse Brigade], married Mary Ingram, in Menen on 15 March 1730. [SB]

GRAHAM, JAMES, a Scot, was married in Bergen op Zoom on 15 August 1714. [WBA]

GRAHAM, MARY, widow of David Hadden a Corporal in Colonel Colyear's Regiment in Flanders, a petition in 1698. [NRS.GD220.6.1749]

GRAHAM, WILLIAM, master of the Owner's Goodwill of Perth trading between Perth and Duinkerken [Dunkirk] in 1765. [NRS.E504.27.5]

GRANT, Colonel ALEXANDER, in Vlaanderen [Flanders], 1709-1710. [NRS.GD248.496.12]

GRANT, Colonel JAMES, at Bergen [Mons], a letter to Colonel William Grant of Ballindalloch, dated on 21 September 1709. [NRS.GD248.18.4.7]

GRANT, JAMES, was promoted to Captain of Major-General James Sinclair's Royal Regiment of Foot, in Vlaanderen [Flanders] on 24 October 1744. [NRAS.771.Bundle 478]

GRAY, JOHN, master of the Post bound for Vlaanderen [Flanders] in January 1598. [XEBR.4.1.1598]

GRAY, JOHN, a Scot, was married in Bergen op Zoom, Brabant, on 28 April 1719. [WBA]

GRAY, JOHN, born in Sluys and baptised in Philipine on 27 September 1767, son of Angus Gray, a Corporal of the 2nd Battalion of Colonel Gordon's Regiment of the Scots Brigade, [De Schotse Brigade], and his wife

Anna Margrit Veldens who married in Nijmegen on 7 August 1764. [SB]

GRAY, ROBERT, a soldier of Lieutenant Colonel Sir Andrew Agnew's Company of the Scots Brigade, [De Schotse Brigade], in Brugge [Bruges] on 13 June 1745. [NRS.GD154.636]

GRAY, WILLIAM, from Aberdeen, then in Vlaanderen [Flanders], was expected to return on 10 July 1540. [ACR.810]

GRAY, WILLIAM, [Guilliame Gree] a Scottish soldier under Captain Phillippe la Lou, married Josijnta Jacobsdochter from Nieuwpoort in Vlaanderen [Flanders], in Leiden on 16 March 1606. [Leiden Marriage Register]

GREGORIE, DAVID, a merchant in Dunkirk versus Archibald Stewart of Orchell, in the Court of Session in Edinburgh, on 4 March 1778. [NRS.CS16.1.173]

GREMAR, EGIDIUS, a tapestry-maker from Arras, was in the service of King James I of Scotland in 1435. [SFP.60]

GRIERSON, WILLIAM, master of the Susanna of Leith, a charter party for a voyage from Dysart or Wemyss, both in Fife, with coal bound for Oostende [Ostend] in 1677. [NRS.AC7.4]

GRIGOR, ROBERT, eldest son of Robert Grigor, a writer [lawyer] Elgin, Moray, died in Antwerp, on 27 May 1854. [IA]

GROSSER, ANDREW, a burgess of Edinburgh in 1599. [EBR][SFP.66]

GUNN, HANNA, daughter of William Gunn, a soldier of Major Bruce's Company of the Scots Brigade, [De Schotse Brigade], and his wife Catherine Fraser, was baptised in Yperen [Ypres] on 31 July 1768. [SB]

GUTHRIE, WILLIAM, a burgess of Dundee, returned there from Vlaanderen [Flanders] in 1611. [RPCS.IX.260]

HACKETT, ROBERT, Lieutenant Colonel of a Scottish Regiment in Flanders in 1690, possibly a Jacobite. [RPCS.XV.1.104]

HAGUE, MATTHIAS, son of Robert Hague, a soldier in Colonel Delat's Company of the Scots Brigade, [De Schotse Brigade], and his wife Janet Wayten, was baptised in Yperen [Ypres] on 25 March 1736. [SB]

HAIR, GEORGE, a Scot, was married in Bergen op Zoom on 23 June 1636. [WBA]

HALYBURTON, ANDREW, a Scots merchant based in the Low Countries, also Conservator of the Scots Privileges there, died in 1507. [LAH][SFP]

HALIBURTON, WILLIAM, an Ensign of Colonel Douglas's Regiment, who probably who fought in Vlaanderen [Flanders], died in Darien, Panama, on 5 September 1698, testament confirmed with the Commissariat of Edinburgh on 8 September 1707. [NRS]

HALKETT, CHARLES, son of Brigadier Charles Halkett of the Scots Brigade, [De Schotse Brigade], and his wife Dame Johanna Margrita Corbet, was baptised at Bergen [Mons] on 25 October 1715. [SB]

HALKETT, GEORGE, Conservator of the Scots Nation in Flanders, sent a quantity of books to King James VI in January 1576. [Accounts of the Treasurer of Scotland, XIIII.]

HALKETT, GEORGE, master of the Heart of Burntisland trading between Kirkcaldy in Fife and Oostende [Ostend] in August 1670. [NRS.E72.9.4]

HALKET, Dr JAMES, in Antwerpen [Antwerp] letters dated 1682. [NRS.GD29.1915]

HALKETT, JOHN, son of Brigadier Charles Halkett of the Scots Brigade, [De Schotse Brigade], and his wife Dame Johanna Margrita Corbet, was baptised at Doornik [Tournai] on 14 February 1794. [SB]

HALKETT, JUDITH, daughter of Brigadier Charles Halkett of the Scots Brigade, [De Schotse Brigade], and his wife Dame Johanna Margrita Corbet, was baptised at Bergen [Mons] on 16 March 1714. [SB]

HALKETT, SUSANNA JUDITH, daughter of Brigadier Charles Halkett of the Scots Brigade, [De Schotse Brigade], and his wife Dame Johanna Margrita Corbet, was baptised at Yperen [Yres] in 1750. [SB]

HAMILTON, Lord GEORGE, born in 1666, died in 1737, son of the Earl of Hamilton; a soldier, fought in the Low Countries and at the Siege of Antwerp, [Antwerpen] also in Brugge, [Bruges], letters dated 1694 and 1706. [NRS.GD406.1.5302 and 7662]

HAMILTON, JAMES, a prisoner, guilty of murder, opted to go to Vlaanderen [Flanders] as a soldier in 1596. [RPCS.VIII.779]

HAMILTON, JAMES, born around 1640 in Murdieston, Fife, a portrait painter in Edinburgh, fled to Brussels, Flanders in 1650s, later in Germany, died 1720. [PS.44]

HAMILTON, JOHN 'is in Brussels with the Duke of Alva', 1570. [CSP.III.94]

HAMILTON, Colonel JOHN, was licenced by King James VI 'to strek drummes and mak proclamatioun in all burghs to recruit fower companies for Flanders' in 1596. [NRS.GD86.318]

HAMILTON, JOHN, in Bergen op Zoom, Brabant, a notarial deed in 1668. [WBA]

HAMILTON NICOLAS, [Claes Hammelton] from Scotland, married Jannetgen Jannsen from 'sGravensbrakels in Vlaanderen, [Flanders], in Leiden on 3 May 1590. [Leiden Marriage Register]

HAMILTON, PATRICK, sent his servant via England to Flanders in 1502. [ATS]

HAMILTON, ROBERT, a Captain of Colonel John Buchan's Regiment of Foot in Vlaanderen [Flanders], a deed dated 1696. [NRS.RD2.79.878]

HAMILTON, THOMAS, from Bathgate, in West Lothian, formerly a Captain of Sir John Mill's Regiment in Vlaanderen [Flanders], later was employed as an overseer at the Scots Company settlement at Darien, Panama, testament confirmed with the Commissariat of Edinburgh in 1707. [NRS]

HAMILTON, WALTER, a Surgeon Lieutenant serving in the War of Austrian Succession, a letter from Gent [Ghent] dated 30 October 1744. [NRS.NRAS.2177.5306; 1339.bundle 50/2]

HAMILTON, WILLIAM, 2nd Duke of Hamilton, in exile, accounts in Antwerpen [Antwerp] and Brussels, around 1649-1650. [NRS.NRAS.332.M14.3.5]

HAMILTON, WILLIAM, an Ensign who probably fought in Vlaanderen [Flanders], died in Darien, Panama, in 1698. [NLS.RY288/19]

HAMILTON, WILLIAM, and Company in Antwerp, a decreet in 1826. [NRS.CS44.115.76]

HAMYLL, JAMES, in Flanders, in 1502. [ATS]

HANSCHEL, Captain, master of the De Jonge Lieffelt from Ghent to Dundee with a cargo of tow in April 1854. [DPCA]

HARPER, JOHN, son of Robert Harper, a soldier of Colonel Halketts Company in the Scots Brigade, [De Schotse Brigade], and Agnes his wife, was baptised in Yperen [Ypres] on 9 July 1752. [SB]

HAY, ANDREW, a soldier of the Scots Brigade, [De Schotse Brigade], married Cathelijne Gisens from Brugge [Bruges] in Leiden on 15 June 1603. [Leiden Marriage Register]

HAY, ALEXANDER, a Scot, was married in Bergen op Zoom on 30 December 1654. [WBA]

HAY, DAVID, a soldier, probably who fought in Vlaanderen [Flanders], died in Darien, Panama, testament confirmed with the Commissariat of Edinburgh in 1707. [NRS]

HAY, FRANCIS, master of the Vos van Brugge [the Fox of Bruges], from Oostende [Ostend] to Leith in 1666 with a cargo of cloth, knitting, Hollands, needles, thimbles, iron, madder, fustick, tow, hops, sugar, pans, whalebone, prunes, starch, white-iron, vinegar, drinking glasses, paper, aniseed, wire, mirrors, shiffon, gum, and cramery. [NRS.E72.15.2]

HAY, FRANCIS, master of the Keysar van Brugge [Caesar of Bruges], arrived in Leith from Oostende [Ostend] in 1666 with a cargo of lint-seed, iron, almonds, soap, sugar, paper, ginger, and cloth. [NRS.E72.15.2]

HAY, HUGH, sometime a Lieutenant of the Earl of Tullibardine's Regiment in Flanders, thereafter in the Service of the Scottish African Company at Darien, Panama, testament confirmed with the Commissariat of Edinburgh in 1707. [NRS]

HAY, JOHN, [Jan Heey], from Scotland, married Grietgen Quaetackers from Pitten in Vlaanderen [Flanders], in Leiden on 21 June 1589. [Leiden Marriage Register]

HAY, ROBERT, a Scot, was married in Bergen op Zoom on 14 April 1626. [WBA]

HAY, ROBERT, of Linphim, in Brussels, accounts in 1823. [NRS.NRAS.2720.827]

HAY, THEODORE, a Lieutenant of Lord George Hamilton's Regiment in Vlaanderen [Flanders], husband of Margaret Smith, a deed dated 1697. [NRS.RD2.81/1.202]

HECTOR, ..., son of Robert Hector a gunmaker in Leith, was sent to Flanders in 1541 to serves as a apprentice gunmaker there. [SFP.66]

HEDEOUX, [or Hedens], SIMON, master of the Lewda van Duinerken a prize ship which was captured by Captain David Alexander, master of the James of Anstruther in Fife in 1626, also during August 1629. [NRS.AC7.1.259; AC7.2] [RPCS.I.283; XIII.740; VI.572]; the cargo of salt was sold to William Dick, a merchant burgess of Edinburgh in 1631. [RPCS.IV.147]

HEFFER, JOHN, a soldier of Lieutenant Colonel Sir Andrew Agnew's Company of the Scots Brigade, [De Schotse Brigade], in Brugge [Bruges] on 13 June 1745. [NRS.GD154.636]

HEGGIE, MATTHEW, master of the Blessing of Kirkcaldy trading between Brugge [Bruges] and Kirkcaldy in Fife in 1681. [NRS.E72.9.11]

HEGS, ROBERT, a gardener, aboard ship in Leith, a recruit for the army in Vlaanderen [Flanders], to be put ashore and imprisoned in Canongait Tolbooth, by order of the Privy Council in 1691. [RPCS.XVI.1.127]

HENRICSON, CORNELIUS, from Niewport in Flanders, in Aberdeen in 1453. [AGC]

HENDERSON, JAMES, a Scottish merchant, was admitted as a burgess of Antwerp in 1537. [SAA]

HENDERSON, WILLIAM, a Captain of Colonel George McGill's Regiment, in Flanders, later a Captain in the Service of the Scots Indian and African Company in Darien, Panama, testament confirmed with the Commissariat of Edinburgh on 7 October 1707. [NRS]

HESSILS, PIERRE, master of the Henrietta van Ostende arrived in Dundee from Ostende on 20 April 1782, also on 6 March 1783. [NRS.E504.11.10]

HIER, JACOB, master of the Draak van Oostende [Griffin of Ostend], from Airth in Stirlingshire with a cargo of coal bound for Brugge [Bruges] in September 1691. [NRS.E72.5.37]

HELY, GEORGE, master of the Haas van Brugge [Hare of Bruges] arrived in Leith from Oostende [Ostend] with a cargo of hops, tow, iron, garden seeds, cloth and ribbons, in March 1666. [NRS.E72.15.2]

HENDERSON, JAMES, was born in Antwerp in 1537. [SAA]

HENDERSON, JAMES, son of William Henderson, a soldier in Captain Graham's Company of the Scots Brigade, [De Schotse Brigade], and Agnes Leslie, his wife, was baptised in Yperen [Ypres] on 25 August 1749. [SB]

HENDERSON, THOMAS, master of the Good Intent of Dundee from Duinkerken [Dunkirk] to Aberdeen in August 1751. [NRS.E504.1.4]

HENDRIX, BROER, a harpooner aboard the North Star of Dunbar arrived in Leith in 1752 from Greenland. [NRS.E508.49.8]

HENDRY, ANDREW, son of James Henry, a soldier in Captain Irons' Company of the Scots Brigade, [De Schotse Brigade], and his wife Elizabeth Low, was baptised in Yperen [Ypres] on 8 May 1736. [SB]

HENRY, JAMES, master of the George of Kirkcaldy trading between Oostende [Ostend] and Kirkcaldy in Fife in 1672. [NRS.E72.9.5]

HENRY, JAMES, a soldier of Captain Irons Company in the Scots Brigade, [De Schotse Brigade], and his wife Elizabeth Low, parents of Andrew Henry, who was baptised in Yperen [Ypres] on 8 May 1736, and Mary baptised in Namur on 23 December 1742. [SB]

HENRYSON, JAMES, [Jacob Henricxon], a Scottish merchant, was admitted as a burgess of Antwerpen [Antwerp] in 1537. [SA. Antwerpen, Poorterboek]

HENRICSON, WILLIAM, a Scot, a linen weaver in Bergen op Zoom, Brabant, an inventory in 1489. [GAR.Inv.3092.34v]

HERBEAN, JACOB, master of the Mary and Joseph of Ostend bound from Limekilns in Fife with a cargo of coal to Ostend in June 1691. [NRS.E72.5.37]

HESSILS, PIETER, master of the Henrietta van Oostende [Henrietta of Ostend] trading between Oostende [Ostend] and Dundee in 1782-1783. [NRS.E504.11.10]

HODGE, JOHN, a Scot, was married in Bergen op Zoom, Brabant, on 15 August 1710. [WBA]

HOGG, INGRAM, a soldier, was granted a pass to travel to Vlaanderen [Flanders] on 1 June 1631. [TNA.E157.15]

HOGG, WILLIAM, married Jean Burn, in Yperen [Ypres] on 28 February 1737. [SB]

HOLLAND, WILLIAM the Earl of, in 1411 permitted Arnot Jokebsen, Dirk Piterson, Cop Lunsea, Keniven etc to make reprisals by sea and land 'against our enemies the Scots. [NNQ.III35]

HOLLEY, HENDRIE, a soldier of Lieutenant Colonel Sir Andrew Agnew's Company of the Scots Brigade, [De Schotse Brigade], in Brugge [Bruges] on 13 June 1745. [NRS.GD154.636]

HOME, Sir ALEXANDER, of Manderston, Master of the Household of the Princess Royal of Orange, and Captain of a Company of Foot in the service of that country, testament confirmed with the Commissariat of Edinburgh on 22 January 1702. [NRS]

HOME, WILLIAM, was before the court in Kales [Calais] re a debt due to Nicolas Calchefier, at 9 am on 11 August 1600. [NRS.JC66.9]

HOOD, ALEXANDER, from Scotland, a soldier under Captain Hay, married Neeltgen Gijsenbaert from Diksmuide in Vlaanderen [Flanders], in Leiden on 23 February 1580. [Leiden Marriage Register]

HOPE, JOHN, [Jan Hop], a merchant from Scotland, was admitted as a burgess of Antwerpen [Antwerp] in 1544. [SA.Antwerpen, Poorterboek]

HOPE, THOMAS, son of Alexander Hope of Kerse, a soldier, probably who fought in Vlaanderen [Flanders], from Leith aboard the Unicorn bound for Darien, Panama, on 14 July 1698, died in Jamaica, testament confirmed with the Commissariat of Edinburgh in 1707. [NRS]

HOWARD, MARY JOSEPH, in Antwerpen [Antwerp] a letter to John Drummond dated 1739. [NRS.GD24.3.390]

HOWITT, JOHN, a soldier of Lieutenant Colonel Sir Andrew Agnew's Company of the Scots Brigade, [De Schotse Brigade], in Brugge [Bruges] on 13 June 1745. [NRS.GD154.636]

HUME, ALEXANDER, Lord Polwarth, in Kales [Calais] a letter dated 1721. [NRS.GD158.1288]

HUME, GEORGE, born 1610, a soldier, was granted a pass to travel to Vlaanderen [Flanders] on 2 July 1635. [TNA.E157.20]

HUME, WILLIAM, an Ensign, married Elizabeth Grant in Yperen [Ypres] on 9 August 1735; parents of Grant Hume who was baptised in Duinkerken [Dunkirk] on 28 March 1736. [SB]

HUNTER, ALEXANDER, a merchant, and four others, was sent to England and Flanders to recruit skilled cloth workers to teach their skills in Edinburgh on 25 February 1601. [EBR]

HUNTER, THOMAS, master of the Bathie of Queensferry bound from Alloa in Stirlingshire with a cargo of coal for Brugge [Bruges] in January 1691. [NRS.E72.5.37]

HUTCHEON, JAMES, master of the Margaret of Kirkcaldy trading between Oostende [Ostend] and Kirkcaldy in Fife in 1665. [NRS.E72.9.1]

HUTCHISON, ROBERT, a soldier of Lieutenant Colonel Sir Andrew Agnew's Company of the Scots Brigade, [De Schotse Brigade], in Brugge [Bruges] on 13 June 1745. [NRS.GD154.636]

HUTTON, DAVID, master of the Cockburn of Dundee, trading between Perth and Duinkerken [Dunkirk] in 1753. [NRS.E504.27.3]

HUTTON, THOMAS, a soldier of Captain Johnstone's Company in the Scots Brigade, [De Schotse Brigade], married Margaret Cattenach, a widow, in Bommel on 12 March 1748. [SB]

HUEYENBUS, PIETER, a harpooner aboard the Campbelltown of Campbelltown in arrived in Campbelltown in Argyll on 28 November 1751, from Greenland. [NRS.E508.48.8]

HYSLOP, RICHARD, a mariner aboard the George of Leith, was imprisoned in Duinkerken [Dunkirk] in 1689. [XEBR.6.11.1689]

INGLIS, ALEXANDER, possibly from Dunblane, a drummer in Captain George Hume's Company of the Scots Brigade, [De Schotse Brigade], married Emmeken Clerkx from Moerbeecke in Vlaanderen [Flanders], in Arnemuiden on 2 June 1612. [Arnrmuiden Marriage Register]

INGLIS, DENIS, was liberated from Edinburgh Tolbooth in 1692 on condition he joined the Earl of Leven's Regiment in Vlaanderen [Flanders]. [NRS.GD26.7.74]

INGLIS, ROBERT, master of the Margaret of Dundee bound for Oostende [Ostend], in 1716-1717. [NRS.E508]

INGRAM, PETER, a soldier of Lieutenant Holbeath's Regiment, married Margaret Thomson, in Breda, on 15 May 1748, parents of Geoge Ingram baptised in Yperen [Ypres] on 22 May 1749, Helen Ingram was baptised in Yperen

[Ypres] on 7 November 1750, and Henry Ingram baptised there on 29 April 1754. [SB]

IRELAND, THOMAS, a soldier, married Jean Pittuloch in Yperen [Ypres] on 10 May 1734, parents of Isabel, baptised at Veuren on 18 April 1735, and Janet baptised in Yperen [Ypres] on 16 January 1737. [SB]

IRONS, CORNELIUS, son of Captain Thomas Irons of the Scots Brigade, [De Schotse Brigade] and his wife Damme Antonnete Van Eck, was baptised in Yperen [Ypres] on 5 December 1736, and John Irons was baptised in Namur on 7 May 1739. [SB]

IRONS, JOHN, an Ensign of Colonel Gordon's Regiment of the Scots Brigade, [De Schotse Brigade], married Josina Maria Vos in Namur on 3 December 1760. [SB]

IRVINE, JAMES, of Drum, Aberdeenshire, a reference by John Leslie, the Bishop of Ross, in a letter to the Governor of the Spanish Netherlands dated 6 June 1596. [State Archives in Brussels] [SNQ.1.59]

IRVINE, JAMES, former clerk of the Canongait, Edinburgh, later on His Majesty's Service in Vlaanderen [Flanders], a petition in 1690. [RPCS.XV.424]

JACKSON, GEORGE, was banished to Flanders for attending religious conventicles in 1686. [NRS.JC39.93]

JACKSON, SYBBILLA, daughter of William Jackson a Sergeant of Captain Douglas's Company in the Scots Brigade, [De Schotse Brigade], and Ann Pringle his wife, was baptised in Yperen [Ypres] on 12 September 1754. [SB]

JAFFRAY, ALEXANDER, Provost of Aberdeen, aboard the Elizabeth of Kirkcaldy at Briel in 1649, a letter for the Conservator of the Scots Privileges. [JTC.191]

JAMART, JACOB, a merchant in Edinburgh in 1674. [EBR]

JAMIESON, JAMES, master of the Unicorn of Queensferry in West Lothian which was captured by a French privateer the Lonoran van Duinkerken in 1703. [NRS.AC9.9]

JAMIESON, JOHN, a soldier of Lieutenant Colonel Sir Andrew Agnew's Company of the Scots Brigade, [De Schotse Brigade], in Brugge [Bruges] on 13 June 1745. [NRS.GD154.636]

JANS, TANNEKEN, from Breda in Brabant, married Thomas Duncan from Edinburgh, in Rotterdam on 2 August 1598. [GAR]

JANSEN, ALBERT, from Calais, [Kales], master of the Jonas van Duinkerken [Dunkirk] which was captured at sea by the Scots in 1628. [NRS.AC7.1.190]

JANSSEN, CORNELIS, in Oostende, [Ostend], a certificate dated 24 December 1665. [NRS.GD68.1.33]

JANSON, JAN, master of the Rood Greihaund van Amsterdam [Red Greyhound of Amsterdam] was attacked by Dunkirk privateers off Aberdeen in 1599. [RPCS.VII.14]

JOHANNIS, CAREL, master of the Catolina van Ostende from Ostende to Dundee in April 1783. [NRS.E504.11.9]

JOHN, stepson of Baldwin the Fleming, settled in Upper Clydesdale at a site now known as Crawfordjohn. [SFP.50]

JOHNS, WILLIAM, son of James Johns a soldier of Captain Boyd's Company in the Scots Brigade, [De Schotse Brigade], and wife Isabel Baillie, was baptised in Namur on 14 July 1737. [SB]

JOHNSON, GEORGE, [Joris Jansz.] from Scotland, a widower and innkeeper, married Marytgen Henricdochter Roosenboom from Antwerpen [Antwerp], the widow of John Thomas of Shetland [Jan Tomas van Hitland] in Leiden on 13 October 1606. [Leiden Marriage Register]

JOHNSON, JOHN, [Jan Janz.] from Scotland, was admitted as a burgess of Bergen op Zoom, Brabant, in 1503. [GAB.Bergen op Zoom]

JOHNSON, JOHN, a Scot, was married in Bergen op Zoom, Brabant, on 1 January 1681. [WBA]

JOHNSON, PETER, a widower from Aberdeen, married Jenneke Adriaens from Wusen in Vlaanderen [Flanders] in Dordrecht on 4 December 1583. [Dordrecht Marriage Register]

JOHNSON, THOMAS, a linen weaver in Bergen op Zoom, an inventory, 1501. [GAB.Inv.3092.62v]

JOHNSON, THOMAS, [Tomas Jansz.] from Scotland, a widower and a cobbler, married Adriaentgen Harings from Proven in Flanders, in Leiden on 28 November 1608. [Leiden Marriage Register]

JOHNSTONE, ALEXANDER, a soldier, probably who fought in Vlaanderen [Flanders], died in Darien, Panama, in 1699, testament confirmed with the Commissariat of Edinburgh in 1707. [NRS]

JOHNSTONE, ISABEL, daughter of James Johnstone, a soldier of Captain Halkett's Company of the Scots Brigade, [De Schotse Brigade], and his wife Margaret, was baptised at Bergen [Mons] in 1713. [SB]

JOHNSTONE, JOHN, of Westerhill, died in Doornik [Tournai] on 30 September 1711.

JOHNSTON, JOHN, a Scot, was married in Bergen op Zoom, Brabant, on 17 January 1714. [WBA]

JOLLIE, Miss CHRISTIAN, in Antwerpen, [Antwerp] died on 14 January 1850, inventory, 1850, Commissariat of Edinburgh. [NRS]

JONKING, DAVID, a merchant, was admitted as a burgess of Edinburgh on 10 January 1610. [Edinburgh Burgess Roll] [SFP.66]

JOP, PIETER, a barber surgeon and apothecary, only son of Pieter Jop a burgess, was admitted as a guilds-brother of Aberdeen on 15 April 1663.[ABR]

JUNKINE, BARTILMO, married Janet Gray from Leith in the Canongait on 31 May 1619. [Canongait Marriage Register]

JUNKINE, JOHN, a mason employed in the construction of Edinburgh Castle in 1615. [AMW.1.379]

KEITH, GEORGE, partner in an Oostende [Ostend] merchant house around 1781. [NRS.GD44.43.257.24]

KELLO, JOHN, a prisoner in Edinburgh Tolbooth, accused of keeping a brothel, was granted to Lieutenant Alexander Dickson to serve as a soldier in Vlaanderen [Flanders] in 1691. [RPCS.XVI.1.657]

KELT, RICHARD, a guilds-brother and burgess of Perth, made payment in Flemish Crowns in the Head Guild Court in Perth Tolbooth on 11 January 1465. [The Perth Guildry Book, 1452-1601; Edinburgh 1993]

KEMP, PETER, master of the *St Eve of Aberdeen* from Wemyss in Fife to Oostende [Ostend] in October 1666. [NRS.E72.9.1]

KENDALL, JAMES, master of the *James*, from Oostende [Ostend] to Leith with a cargo of iron, madder, hemp, figs, tobacco, hops, cloth, seeds, almonds, sugar, wire, sugar, oil and currants in 1665. [NRS.E72.15.2]

KEIRIE, Sir CHARLES, commander of a Scottish Regiment in Flanders in 1690. [RPCS.XV.104]

KENNEDY, AGNES, daughter of William Kennedy a soldier of Captain Irons' Company of the Scots Brigade, [De Schotse Brigade], and his wife Elizabeth McBain, was baptised in Namur on 6 January 1739, daughter Margaret was baptised there in December 1742, Jean was baptised in Namur on 7 January 1745, and their brother William Kennedy was baptised in Yperen [Ypres] on 6 September 1750. [SB]

KENNEDY, JAMES, sent a letter from Kales [Calais] complaining of the unjust dues being levied on Scottish ships at Brugge, [Bruges], in 1665. [NRAS.464.19]

KENNEDY, JAMES, in Brussels in 1677. [NRS.GD149.332]

KENNEDY, JEAN, daughter of William Kennedy a soldier in Captain Iron's Company of the Scots Brigade, [De Schotse Brigade], and his wife Elizabeth McBain, was baptised in Yperen [Ypres] on 11 May 1749. [SB]

KENNEDY, WILLIAM, son of William Kennedy a soldier in Captain Iron's Company of the Scots Brigade, [De Schotse Brigade], and his wife Elizabeth McBain, was baptised in Yperoe [Ypres] on 6 September 1750. [SB]

KENNEDY, ..., a soldier in Vlaanderen [Flanders], husband of Margaret Morrison in Ayr in 1696. [NRS.CH2.751.8/139]

KENNERS, LIVINA E., in Vlaanderen [Flanders] a deed in 1877. [NRS.RD5.1619.17]

KERR, DANIEL, of Kersland, a Major of the Earl of Angus's Regiment in Vlaanderen [Flanders], was admitted as a burgess and guilds-brother of Ayr on 11 January 1692. [Ayr Burgess Roll]

KERR, Lord JOHN, possibly a student at Leiden, a letter to his mother stating his intent to visit Brabant, later as a soldier a letter, dated 10 September 1694, to his father, the Marquis of Lothian, stating that he was to winter at the side of a canal between Gent [Ghent] and Brugge [Bruges]. [NRS.GD40.2.7.64; 2.3.14-157]

KIDD, GEORGE, son of George Kidd a soldier in Major Nicolson's Company of the Scots Brigade, [De Schotse Brigade], and his wife Agnes Christie, was baptised in Namur on 18 November 1742. [SB]

KING, MARIA, daughter of John King a Sergeant of Captain Dodsworth's Company of the Scots Brigade, [De Schotse Brigade], and his wife Mary Clair, was baptised in Yperen [Ypres] on 13 November 1734, her sister Anna King was baptised there on 24 February 1737. [SB]

KINLOCH, CHARLES, of the 7th Fusiliers in Vlaanderen [Flanders], a letter dated 11 July 1815. [NRS.GD453.164]

KINNAIRD, ..., son of the laird of Culbin, an Ensign who probably fought in Flanders, died in Darien, Panama, in 1700. [DD.325]

KINNINMONT, ALEXANDER, from Edinburgh, was married in Bergen op Zoom, Braband, on 20 August 1718. [WBA]

KIRKPATRICK, JOHN, formerly of the Earl of Argyll's Regiment in Vlaanderen [Flanders] a Lieutenant at the Scots settlement at Darien, Panama, in 1699, testament confirmed with the Commissariat of Edinburgh in 1707. [NRS]

KIRKPATRICK, JOHN, a merchant in Oostende, [Ostend] eldest son of William Kirkpatrick in 1784. [NRS.CS97.111.18; CS228.MC6.27.2]

KNIFTE, FRANCIS, a merchant in Antwerpen, [Antwerp] freighted the St Francis van Antwerpen to sail from Oostende [Ostend] via Dublin bound for Scotland, which was shipwrecked near Portpatrick in Scotland in 1666. [NRS.RH9.5.31]

KNIGHT, GEORGE, a mariner burgess of Dundee, master of the Jonas trading with Vlaanderen [Flanders] in 1612 and 1613. [DSL]

KNIGHT, ROBERT, former cashier of the South Sea Company, escaped from prison in Antwerpen [Antwerp] in 1721. [NRS.GD112.44.4]

KNOX, JOHN, a Scot, was married in Bergen op Zoom, Brabant, on 14 September 1685. [WBA]

KYLL, JAMES, master of the James and John of Dundee bound from Dundee for Duinkerken [Dunkirk] in August 1682. [NRS.E72.7.9]

LAING, WILLIAM, a soldier of Captain Mackenzie's Company of the Scots Brigade, [De Schotse Brigade], married Marie Muschet in Namur on 22 January 1741, parents of Isobel Laing baptised there on 2 April 1743. [SB]

LAMB, ALEXANDER, a Scot, was married in Bergen op Zoom, Brabant, on 26 August 1733. [WBA]

LAMBERTON, WILLIAM, son of John Lamberton, a Corporal in Colonel Halkett's Company of the Scots Brigade, [De Schotse Brigade], and his wife Agnes Francis, was baptised in Namur on 21 November 1740, also their daughter Isabel was baptised there on 7 January 1743. [SB]

LAMBIN, a Fleming who settled in Upper Lanarkshire before 1200, at a site named Lamington. [SFP.50][KS.289]

LAMOND, DUNCAN, a Scot, was married in Bergen op Zoom, Brabant, on 29 February 17.. [WBA]

LAMPSINS, CORNELIUS, and his wife Maria Meunicx in Oostende, were parents of Cornelius and Adrian Lampsins merchants in Middelburg and Vlissingen [Flushing], supplied arms and ammunition to the Scots Armies in the 1640s. [JTC.XXVI]

LANG, THOMAS, son of John Lang, a soldier in Captain Irons Company of the Scots Brigade, [De Schotse Brigade], and his wife Euphan Hutchison, was baptised in Yperen [Ypres] on 17 May 1734. [SB]

LAUDER, GEORGE, a Sergeant of Lieutenant Colonel Sir Andrew Agnew's Company of the Scots Brigade, [De Schotse Brigade], in Brugge [Bruges] on 13 June 1745. [NRS.GD154.636]

LAUSON, JAMES, in Gent, [Ghent], a letter to Lady Pilmor, dated 9 October 1707. [NRS.GD214.699]

LAWS, PETER, master of the Hope which arrived in Leith from Vlaanderen [Flanders] in January 1666 with a cargo of onions. [NRS.E72.15.2]

LAWSON, Dr ISAAC, physician to the British Hospital in Vlaanderen [Flanders], testament, 25 February 1778, Commissariat of Edinburgh. [NRS]

LAWSON, JAMES, a Captain of Colonel George Prestoun's Regiment in Vlaanderen [Flanders] a deed dated 1707. [NRS.RD4.100.232]

LAWSON, WILLIAM, from Edinburgh, an Ensign who probably fought in Vlaanderen [Flanders] died at Darien in Panama in 1699, testament was confirmed in 1707 with the Commissariat of Edinburgh. [NRS]

LEITCH, ALEXANDER, from Aberdeen, then in Vlaanderen [Flanders], expected to return on 10 July 1540. [AC]

LEATHES, WILLIAM, in Brussels, letters to Lord Polworth from 1716 until 1722. [NRS.GD15534]

LE SAGHER, JOHN, and some other Flemings took three ships bound from Hull for Brabant to Aberdeen where they left the merchants before heading for Flanders where they sold the cargoes in 1313. [CDS.V.584]

LESH, HANS, a tavernier or innkeeper from Aberdeen, was admitted as a burgess of Antwerpen [Antwerp] in 1589. [SA.Antwerpen Poorterboek]

LESLIE, JOHN, a Sergeant of Captain Orrock's Company of the Scots Brigade, [De Schotse Brigade], married Margaret Black in Charleroi on 19 January 1743, parents of John Alexander Leslie who was baptised in Yperen [Ypres] on 2 June 1749. [SB]

LESLEY, WILLIAM, master of the Marjory of Montrose from Montrose to Dunkirk on 1 September 1749. [NRS.E504.24.2]; from Montrose in Angus to Dunkirk on 25 October 1749. [NRS.CE53.1.4]

LESTER, SARA, daughter of Benjamin Lester a soldier of General Graham's Company of the Scots Brigade, [De Schotse Brigade], and his wife Jean Baxter, was baptised in Yperen [Ypres] on 7 November 1750. [SB]

LE VENES, ADRIAN, master of the St Jan van Brugge [St John of Bruges] which arrived in Leith from Oostende [Ostend] with a cargo of wine and allum, in April 1666. [NRS E72.15.2]

LIDDLE, JOHN, a soldier of Lieutenant Colonel Sir Andrew Agnew's Company of the Scots Brigade, [De Schotse Brigade], in Brugge [Bruges] on 13 June 1745. [NRS.GD154.636]

LILLIE, ANDREW, a soldier of Major Nicholson's Company of the Scots Brigade, [De Schotse Brigade], married Margret Gravell, in Namur on 19 July 1742. [SB]

LINDSAY, ANDREW, a skipper, returned to Dundee on 20 April 1686 from Dunkirk. [DCA.GD.Hu.SF/3/1]

LINDSAY, JAMES, in Brugge [Bruges] and Utrecht, letters dated from 1691 until 1693. [NRS.NRAS.859.51.16]

LINDSAY, Major JOHN, possibly fought in Flanders before 1697, enlisted in the Scots Darien Company, was bound via Greenock to Darien, Panama, in 1699, was killed there on 30 March 1700. [DD.317] [NRS.GD406.1]

LINDSAY, MARGARET, daughter of John Lindsay a Corporal of Colonel Young's Company of the Scots Brigade, [De Schotse Brigade], and his wife Hermina Livens, was baptised in Yperen [Ypres] on 29 June 1754. [SB]

LINLITHGOW, WILLIAM, a mariner aboard the John of Leith from Vlaanderen [Flanders] to Leith in September 163,1. [SJC.1.206]

LITTLE, ANDREW, a soldier of Lieutenant Colonel Sir Andrew Agnew's Company of the Scots Brigade, [De Schotse Brigade], in Brugge [Bruges] on 13 June 1745. [NRS.GD154.636]

LIVINGSTONE, ALEXANDER, an Ensign of General Halket's Regiment in Flanders, testament confirmed with the Commissariat of Edinburgh on 27 November 1741. [NRS]

LOANIE, PETER, master of the Maria van Duinkerken [Mary of Dunkirk], arrived from Dunkirk in Aberdeen in October 1751. [NRS.E504.1.4]

LOCCARD, SIMON, a Fleming who settled in Upper Lanarkshire before 1200, at a site named Symington. [SFP.50]

LOCCARD, STEPHEN, a Fleming who settled in Dumfriesshire before 1200, at a site named Lockerbie. [SFP.50]

LOCKHART, GEORGE, of Carnwath, Lanarkshire, a Jacobite in exile, in Antwerp on 6 May 1727, a letter to the Old Pretender, [LGL.V.304]; in Brussels, a letter to the Earl of Eglinton, dated 10 June 1727. [NRS.GD3.5.595]

LOCKHART, JACOBA, daughter of Mark Lockhart and his wife Catherine, was baptised in Yperen [Ypres] on 15 October 1769. [SB]

LOCKHART, JAMES, a Lieutenant Colonel of Colonel Halkett's Regiment in Dutch Service, died in Furnes [Veurne] on 26 October 1749. [AJ.98]

LOGAN, ANDREW, a soldier who possibly fought in Flanders, a Sergeant at Darien, Panama in 1699. [DD.262]

LOGAN, JAMES, a Scot, was married in Bergen op Zoom, Brabant, on 14 May 1719. [WBA]

LOLLING, GERRET SAMUEL, a harpooner aboard the Argyll of Campbelltown in arrived in Campbelltown in Argyll on 28 September 1751, from Greenland. [NRS.E508.48.8]

LORENTS, BOOIJ, a harpooner aboard the City of Aberdeen, arrived in Aberdeen on 18 June 1754. from Greenland. [NRS.E508.51.8]

LOSSIER, CLAUS, a Flemish shearer, settled in Dundee around 1601. [SFP.66]

LOTHIAN, WILLIAM, Earl of, in Brussels and Antwerp, see Journal from 1641 to 1650. [NRS.GD40.15.58]

LOUDOUN, JOHN, master of the Jonas of Kirkcaldy in Fife, trading between Vlaanderen [Flanders] and Aberdeen in 1613. [ASW.78]

LOVIE, WILLIAM, master of the Two Friends of Forres trading and smuggling between Duinkerken [Dunkirk] and Leith in 1784. [AJ]

LOW, ..., master of the Providence of Aberdeen trading between Aberdeen and Duinkerken [Dunkirk] in 1751. [AJ]

LOW, ..., master of the Magdalene of Aberdeen, arrived in Aberdeen from Ostend in June 1755. [AJ.387]

LOYODA, DAVID, master of the Stampor van Oostende, arrived in Kirkcaldy in Fife, from Oostende [Ostend] in August 1670. [NRS.E72.9]

LUMSDEN, JAMES, in Oostende, [Ostend], about to join the Duke of York's army, a letter dated 30 April 1794. [NRAS.771.266]

LYON, CHARLES, a Scot, was married in Bergen op Zoom, Brabant, on 30 June 1734. [WBA]

LYON, JOHN, a soldier who was granted a pass to travel to Vlaanderen [Flanders] on 10 August 1632. [TNA.E157.16]

LYON, PETER, son of Robert Lyon a soldier in Captain Irons' Company, of the Scots Brigade, [De Schotse Brigade], and his wife Janet Tate, was baptised in Mechelen [Malines] on 24 April 1746. [SB]

MACALESTER, JOHN, a soldier of Lieutenant General Murray's Regiment, married Pitternella de Long, daughter of Paulus de Long from Tergowes, in Yperen [Ypres] on 28 August 1716. [SB]

MCCAIN, JAMES, a soldier of Lieutenant Colonel Sir Andrew Agnew's Company of the Scots Brigade, [De Schotse Brigade], in Brugge [Bruges] on 13 June 1745. [NRS.GD154.636]

MACCARTNEY, ..., at Oostende, [Ostend] a letter to a friend in London, dated December 1712. [NRS.NRAS.332.M3.11]

MCCELTER, DUNCAN, a Scot, was married in Bergen op Zoom, Brabant, on 22 April 1626. [WBA]

MACCONACHIE, ALEXANDER, son of John Major MacConachie [McOnighie], a soldier of Major Alexander's Company, in the Scots Brigade, [De Schotse Brigade], and his wife, Margaret, was baptised in Yperen [Ypres] on 12 September 1753. [SB]

MCCONNELL, DAVID, a Scot, was married in Bergen op Zoom, Brabant, on 7 October 1733. [WBA]

MACDONALD, ARCHIBALD, a labourer from Leslie in Fife, a private soldier of the 78th Regiment, died in the Regimental Hospital in Brussels on 30 January 1816. [H78.140]

MACDONALD, DONALD, a labourer from Creich, Sutherland, a private soldier of the 78th Regiment, died on 28 October 1815 in hospital at Ostend. [H78.140]

MACDONALD, JOHN, a Sergeant of Captain MacLean's Company of the Scots Brigade, [De Schotse Brigade], married Clara Clark, a widow, in Doornik [Tournai] on 15 May 1722. [SB]

MCDOUGALL, P. and J., calico printers in Glasgow, trading with Brussels, sederunt book 1834-1837. [NRS.CS96.4273]

MCEWAN, MARY, daughter of John McEwan in Bergen op Zoom, married Donald Fraser, son of Alexander Fraser in Inverness-shire, in the Scots Kirk of Rotterdam on 6 September 1719. [RA]

MCFARLANE, PETER, a merchant in Aberdeen, trading with Antwerpen [Antwerp] in 1824. [NRS.CS96.1252]

MCGILL, Major, at Leith aboard ship with recruits bound for [Vlaanderen] Flanders in 1691. [RPCS.XVI.1.127]

MCGOUNE, JOHN, a Sergeant of the Earl of Angus's Regiment in Vlaanderen [Flanders], was admitted as a burgess and guilds-brother of Ayr on 11 January 1692. [Ayr Burgess Roll]

MCHENRY or MCKENDRICK, Lieutenant WILLIAM, in camp near Lille, a letter re the death of Lieutenant Colonel William Shairp, dated in September 1708, [NRS.GD30.1756]; a Lieutenant of the British Fusiliers Regiment, at Gent, [Ghent] letters dated 11 February 1709. [NRS.GD30.1758-1759]

MCILVAINE, PATRICK, a Captain of the Royal Regiment of Foot, died in Flanders, probate in 1695, Prerogative Court of Canterbury. [TNA]

MACINTOSH, KENNETH, from Durness in Caithness, formerly of the 46th Regiment, a Sergeant of the Gordon Highlanders, was killed at Egmont-op-Zee in 1799. [HGH.27]

MCINTOSH, LACHLAN, a soldier of Lieutenant Colonel Sir Andrew Agnew's Company of the Scots Brigade, [De Schotse Brigade], in Brugge [Bruges] on 13 June 1745. [NRS.GD154.636]

MCINTOSH, THOMAS, from Kellochie in Inverness-shire, formerly a Lieutenant of the Earl of Tullibardine's Regiment in Vlaanderen, [Flanders], died at Darien, Panama, in 1699, testament confirmed with the Commissariat of Edinburgh in 1707. [NRS]

MCINTOSH, Miss, youngest daughter of William McIntosh in Grenada, married the Chevalier le Sieur de Colleville, a French Infantry officer, son of Marchioness de Colleville in Normandy, France, in 1791 in Oostende [Ostend] Flanders. [GM.61.1061]

MACKAY, DANIEL, a Scot, was married in Bergen op Zoom, Brabant, on 12 November 1698. [WA]

MACKAY, DONALD, son of Aeneas Mackay, Colonel of a Scots Regiment in Dutch Service, was killed at Doornik [Tournai] in 1745. [BM]

MACKAY, HUGH, third son of Mackay of Scourie, an officer of the Scots Brigade in the Service of the Netherlands, later of Dunbarton's Regiment in the Service of King Louis XIV of France, Army Commander in Scotland, fought at the Battle of Killiecrankie in Perthshire on 27 July 1689, and at the Siege of Dunkeld in Perthshire on 21 August 1689, was killed at the Battle of Steinkirk in Flanders on 3 August 1692. [BM]

MACKAY, HUGH, a labourer from Forgue, Sutherland, a private soldier of the 2nd Battalion of the 78th Regiment of Foot, was drowned at Nieupoort, Flanders on 25 July 1815. [H78.140]

MACKAY, JOHN, a labourer from Thurso, Caithness, a private soldier of the 2nd Battalion of the 78th Regiment of Foot, was drowned at Nieupoort, Flanders on 15 July 1815. [H78.140]

MACKAY, ROBERT, a soldier, at Moulin near Namur, a letter to Lord Breadalbane on 12 August 1695. [NRS.GD112.39.171.173]

MCKAY, Sergeant, an inventory of his knapsack, at Antwerpen [Antwerp] in 1745. [NRS.GD26.9.485]

MCKELL, JOHN, a peutherer [pewterer] in Canongait, aboard ship in Leith, a recruit for the army in Vlaanderen [Flanders], to be out ashore and imprisoned in Canongait Tolbooth, by order of the Privy Council in 1691. [RPCS.XVI.1.127]

MCKENZIE, ALEXANDER, possibly formerly a soldier in Vlaanderen [Flanders], enlisted with the Scots Darien Company, died in the West Indies, testament confirmed with the Commissariat of Edinburgh in 1707. [NRS]

MCKENZIE, JOHN, a Scot, was married in Bergen op Zoom, Brabant, on 24 February 1734. [WBA]

MACKENZIE, JOHN, master of the Fortrose of Leith from Aberdeen to Brugge [Bruges] in December 1749. [NRS.E504.1.3]

MACKIE, ALEXANDER, a merchant in Aberdeen, trading with Antwerp in 1821. [NRS.CS96.1252]

MACKISON, JOHN, a Scot, was married in Bergen op Zoom, Brabant, on 13 June 1759. [WBA]

MCLEOD, DONALD, a Captain of Colonel Aeneas Mackay's Regiment in Flanders, a sasine dated 1696. [NRS.RD36.6.167/463]

MCLEOD, HUGH, a merchant in Kingston, Jamaica, partner of John Miller and John Ure in Glasgow, also Joseph Downie in Aux Cayes, Haiti, trading with Antwerp between 1815 and 1819. [NRS.CS96.2311]

MCMILLAN, JOHN, a soldier of Lieutenant Colonel Sir Andrew Agnew's Company of the Scots Brigade, [De Schotse Brigade], in Brugge [Bruges] on 13 June 1745. [NRS.GD154.636]

MABON, ALEXANDER, from Edinburgh, a sword burnisher in Gorkum, married Maycken van Haelemis from Vlaanderen [Flanders], in Leiden on 28 January 1605. [LMR]

MABON, JONAS, from Edinburgh, a sword-burnisher in Gorkum, married Maycken from Tielt in Vlaanderen [Flanders] in Leiden on 17 November 1604. [LMR]

MAIN, GEORGE, a soldier from St Andrews in Fife, married Margaret Brand from Aberdeen, in Geertruidenberg in 1638. [Geertruidenberg Marriage Register]

MAITLAND, JAMES, son and heir of William Maitland secretary to Mary, Queen of Scots, disposed of the lands and barony of Bolton, via a charter subscribed in Antwerp on 15 May 1613. [RGS.VII.897]

MARJINER, GOTTFRIED, a harpooner aboard the Dundee of Dundee, arrived in Dundee in 1754 from Greenland. [NRS.E508.51.8]

MARKIE, WALTER, master of the Marie of Kirkcaldy in Fife trading between Kirkcaldy and Brugge [Bruges] with cargoes of coal in 1681 and 1683. [NRS.E72.14/15]

MARR, JOHN, master of the Providence of Dundee arrived in Dundee from Duinkerken [Dunkirk] in December 1683. [NRS.E72.7.6]

MARSHALL, JAMES, secretary to the Duke of Albany in Scotland, a letter to Raphael de Medici in Antwerp, re Bruges or Middelburg or Veere as a Scottish staple port, dated on 26 September 1520. [NRS.RH1.858]

MARSHALL, ROBERT, master of the Jean of Queensferry from Oostende [Ostend] to Leith in March 1672. [NRS.E72.15.12]; testament, 1679, Commissariat of Edinburgh. [NRS]

MARSS, JAN, master of the Sonnediepgang van Brugge [Sundraught of Bruges] from Carriden, Stirlingshire, with a cargo of coal bound for Flanders in June 1691. [NRS.E72.5.37]

MARTIN, HENRY, master of the Charlotte of Calais, captured the City of Hamburg, master Henry Haridshell, with cargo of Philip van Porten a merchant in Hamburg, bound for Archangel, in 1674. [NRS.HCAS.AC7.5]

MARTIN, JOHN, [Jan Meyerton], a Scottish tailor, was admitted as a citizen of Antwerpen [Antwerp] in 1502. [SA.Antwerpen, Poorterboek]

MARTIN, PETER, a Scottish soldier in Leiden, Holland, married Griete Jansdochter from Antwerp [Antwerpen] in Leiden on 15 March 1591. [Leiden Marriage Register]

MARTIN, WILLIAM, a Scot, was married in Bergen op Zoom, Brabant, on 17 January 1658. [WBA]

MATHESON, ANDREW, was reimbursed for expenses incurred in Flanders in 1504, was there on board the ship of George Patterson from Leith. [ATS]

MAULT, DERRICK, master of the Fortune of Ostend, a privateer, owned by a Dane, captured two Scottish ships and took them to Ostend in 1645, was later captured by the Hunter of London and taken to Kinsale, Ireland, in October 1646. [TNA.HCA.15.2.773]

MAXWELL, JOHN, Earl of Morton, was licenced to go to Flanders for up to five years on 24 August 1584. [RPSS.VIII.2346]

MAXWELL, Lieutenant, of Lieutenant Colonel Sir Andrew Agnew's Company of the Scots Brigade, [De Schotse Brigade] in Brugge [Bruges] on 13 June 1745. [NRS.GD154.636]

MAYLES, JOHN, a soldier of Lieutenant Colonel Sir Andrew Agnew's Company of the Scots Brigade, [De Schotse Brigade], in Brugge [Bruges] on 13 June 1745. [NRS.GD154.636]

MAYNARD the Fleming, planned the layout of Berwick-on-Tweed and later St Andrews in the twelfth century. [SFP]

MEASON, WILLIAM, a skipper trading between Vlaanderen [Flanders] and Aberdeen in 1599, [ASW.44]

MEEK, ALEXANDER, master of the William of Kirkcaldy in Fife, trading between Kirkcaldy and Brugge [Bruges] in 1682. [NRS.E72.9.13]

MEEK, JOHN, master of the David of Kirkcaldy in Fife, trading between Kirkcaldy and Brugge [Bruges] also Oostende [Ostend] in1683. [NRS.E72.9.13]

MENZIES, ANDREW, from Aberdeen, then in Flanders, expected to return on 10 July 1540. [ACR.810]

MENZIES, DAVID, was despatched by Aberdeen Town Council to Flanders to purchase a ship full of salt and to freight a ship back to Aberdeen in 1449. [ACA]

MERCER, JOHN, a merchant burgess of Perth, trading in Flanders in 1328, Ambassador of Scotland in the negotiations for the release of King David II who had been captured after the Battle of Neville's Cross in 1346, in 1360 John Mercer was appointed deputy of the King of Scotland in Flanders, later was Baron of Meiklour in Perthshire. [SFP.59][David II, pp.296/344]

MERCER, Lieutenant Colonel ROBERT, in Antwerpen [Antwerp] a letter dated 1814. [NRS.GD172.1169]

MERCHISTON, Mr JAMES, in Flanders in 1502, linked with the king's forthcoming marriage, had his expenses reimbursed. [ATS]; he was sent to Flanders by the king in 1505. [ATS]

MERSCHALE, THOMAS, a webster [weaver], was admitted as a guilds-brother of Perth on 18 August 1459. [PKA]

MERSTOUN, JOHN, formerly a Lieutenant of Lord Lindsay's Regiment in Vlaanderen [Flanders], thereafter in the service of the Darien Company, in Panama, testament, 11 September 1707, Comm. Edinburgh. [NRS]

MILLER, FRANCIS, born in Antwerpen [Antwerp] in 1841, a hawker residing in the High Street of Glasgow, was accused of assault in 1884. [NRS.AD14.84.45]

MILLER, JOHN, and JOHN URE, merchants in Glasgow, trading with Antwerpen [Antwerp] from 1815 to 1829. [NRS.CS96.2311]

MILLER, ROBERT, of Sir Thomas Livingstone's Regiment in Flanders, husband of Margaret Miller in Lanark, testament confirmed on 7 June 1697 with the Commissariat of Lanark. [NRS]

MILLS, WILLIAM, master of the Providence of Peterhead in Aberdeenshire, trading between Perth and Duinkerken [Dunkirk] in 1767. [NRS.E504.27.5]

MITCHELL, ANDREW, a skipper in Leith, master of the Ewauld which was captured by a Dunkirk man o'war and taken the Newhaven [LeHavre] in France to be sold. In 1618 the ship was retaken by Scots near Wynnefiord in Norway bound with a cargo of timber for Dunkirk. [NRS HCAS.AC7.1.212]

MITCHELL, ROBERT, born 1603, a soldier who was granted a pass to travel to Vlaanderen [Flanders] on 21 February 1628. [TNA.E157.4]

MITCHELL, WILLIAM, a tailor from Calder, Nairn, a private soldier of the 2nd Battalion of the 78th Regiment of Foot, was drowned at Nieupoort, Flanders on 25 July 1815. [H78.140]

MITCHELL, WALTER, a merchant of Antwerpen, [Antwerp], a debtor of John de Vas, an alderman of Aberdeen, a deed dated 30 July 1446. [Aberdeen Council Register #714]

MOFFAT, JOHN, and his son Erasmus Moffat, in Flanders In 1539. [RPSS.2.3116]

MOIR, GEORGE, master of the Charles of Peterhead in Aberdeenshire, trading with Vlaanderen [Flanders] in 1613. [ASW.75]

MOIR, JOHN, master of the Elphinstone of Aberdeen from Brugge [Bruges] to Aberdeen in February 1686. [NRS.E72.1.16]

MONCREIFF, DAVID, formerly an Ensign of the Earl of Tullibardine's Regiment in Vlaanderen [Flanders], Deputy Assistant at Darien, Panama, testament confirmed with the Commissariat of Edinburgh in 1707. [NRS]

MONCREIFF, Colonel Sir JAMES, his Regiment of Foot was bound for Flanders in April 1694, vouchers. [NRS.E94.15]

MONCUR, JAMES, master of the James of Dundee arrived in Dundee from Vlaanderen [Flanders] in November 1617. [DSL]

MONRO, HUGH, formerly a Lieutenant of Lord Murray's Regiment in Vlaanderen [Flanders], an overseer at Darien, Panama, in 1698, testament confirmed with the Commissariat of Edinburgh in 1707. [NRS]

MONTEITH, GEORGE, a merchant in Leith, trading with Flanders in 1660. [NRS.E72]

MONTEITH, JOHN, son of Robert Monteith a merchant in Edinburgh, died in Flanders in 1666. [EBR]

MONTGOMERY, HUGH, of Borland, formerly a Corporal of the Earl of Eglin's troop in Vlaanderen [Flanders], later in Captain Andrew Stewart's Company in Darien, Panama, died there. [APS.14.app.114/127]73]

MONTGOMERIE, ..., in Breda, Brabant, a letter in 1650. [NRS.GD3.5.4.4]

MORAY, GEORGE, Bishop of, and his servants John Reid, John Somerville, John Livingstone, and James Douglas, were licenced to go to Flanders etc on 28 November 1584. [RPSS.VIII.2606]

MORRIS, DAVID, a Scot, was married in Halsteren, Brabant, on 2 March 1678.[WBA]

MORRIS, JOHN, a Scottish tailor in Bergen op Zoom, Brabant, an inventory in 1513. [GAB.Inv.3092.105r]

MORRISON, GEORGE, born 1797 in Banff, son of John Morrison and his wife Ann Longmure, enlisted in the 78th Regiment in 1810, served in Flanders for three years and fought at the Battle of Merexem and at the Siege of Antwerp, he died at Keith in Banffshire on 11 December 1858. [H78.112]

MORTON, WALTER, master of the Antelope of Burntisland in Fife, trading with Brugge [Bruges] and Vlaanderen [Flanders] between 1589 and 1600. [NRS.RH9.1.5]

MOSSMAN, JOHN, a potingar [apothecary] was sent to Flanders by the king in 1504. [ATS]

MUDIE, DAVID, master of the Jean of Limekilns in Fife, from Duinkerken [Dunkirk]] to Aberdeen in December 1750. [NRS.E504.1.3]

MUDIE, HENRY, master of the George of Dundee from Vlaanderen [Flanders] to Dundee in November 1617. [DSL]

MUIR, ALEXANDER, master of the Catto of Burntisland in Fife, from Brugge [Bruges] with a cargo of hards and tow on 18 March 1670. [NRS.E29.9]

MUIR, WILLIAM, a soldier under Captain Balfour in the Ostend Garrison in Flanders, married Jannetgen Jans of Leiden in Holland, there on 15 March 1602. [Leiden Marriage Register]

MUNRO, ROBERT, a letter from Robert Munro to Alexander Brodie, the Lord Lyon, with a list of deserters from Lord Sempill's Regiment, dated at Gent [Ghent] on 22 June 1743. [NRS.NRAS.770. Box 2, bundle 5]

MURDOCH, WILLIAM, servant to James Cunningham a farmer in Waughtoun, aboard ship in Leith, a recruit for the army in Vlaanderen [Flanders], to be put ashore and imprisoned in Canongait Tolbooth, by order of the Privy Council in 1691. [RPCS.XVI.1.127]

MURE, ALEXANDER, master of the Cato of Burntisland, Fife, trading between Kirkcaldy and Brugge [Bruges] in 1670. [NRS.E72.9.4]

MURRAY, ALEXANDER, of Drumdewan, third son of Sir William Murray of Tullibardine, Perthshire, a Colonel in Dutch Service, was killed at Bommel on19 May 1599. [SP.I.466]

MURRAY, Captain DAVID, of Hillfield, purchased a 54 ton boat 'the Mellingill' in Brugge, [Bruges] which he brought to Banff in 1581, however his wife Janet Wemyss complained on 25 February 1581 that John Douglas in Aberdeen and John Fordyce had confiscated the ship [RPCS.III.359]

MURRAY, JAMES, son of Anne Graeme, Lady Abercairny, serving with the army in Bruges and later in camp in Flanders, letters in 1693 and 1694. [NRS.GD24.1.369]

MURRAY, JAMES, of Abercairny, wounded at the Battle of Waterloo in 1815, sent a letter from Brussels. [NRS.GD24.1.374]

MURRAY, JOHN, a burgess of Aberdeen, master of the Susanna from Aberdeen on 6 July 1588, with a cargo of salmon bound for Dieppe from there via Bordeaux to 'myddelsburg in flanderis' then to Spain, when the shipmaster and crew -John Stirling from Torry in Aberdeen,

Thomas Myll there, Alexander Knollis a burgess of Aberdeen, and John Gardner a mariner, were accused of being Protestants and Lutherans, who were then burnt, hung, or became slaves. [ABR. Testimonials]

MURRAY, JOHN, in Oostende [Ostend], a letter to his mother Anna Stewart dated 1678. [NRAS.258.3.1.13]

MURRAY, JOHN, son of Sir Robert Murray of Abercairny, a letter from Brugge [Bruges] in 1694 to his mother Lady Abercairny. John Murray died and was buried in the Monastery of the Irish in Brugge [Bruges] around 1710. [NRS.GD24.1.369/762.4]

MURRAY, JOHN, 2nd Earl of Dunmore, a letter from Richard Basset in Brugge [Bruges] dated 25 August 1742. [NRS.RH4.195.2]

MURRAY, ROBERT, a Lieutenant General in Dutch Service, Governor of Doornik [Tournai], in Flanders, testament confirmed with the Commissariat of Edinburgh on 18 September 1719. [NRS]

MURRAY, Lieutenant Colonel WALTER, in Busch, Brabant, 1669, father of Alexander Murray. [NRS.S/H]

MURRAY, Captain, master of the Beggar's Benison of MacDuff trading between Ostend in Flanders and Aberdeen in 1785. [AJ.1949]

NAIRN, ALEXANDER, master of the Dauphine of Montrose arrived in Montrose, Angus, in October 1682 from Duinkerken [Dunkirk]. [NRS.E72.16.8]

NAIRNE, ALEXANDER, in Kortrijk [Courtrai] a letter dated 29 March 1771 to Robert Forbes of Balinshoe. [NRS.GD68.2.113]

NAIRN, JAMES, master of the Margaret of Elie in Fife, trading with Brugge [Bruges] in 1682. [NRS.E72.13]

NANNIK, ..., an embroiderer arrived in Scotland from Flanders in 1503. [ATS]

NEILSON, ALEXANDER, a Scot, was married in Bergen op Zoom, Brabant, on 13 June 1717. [WBA]

NELSON, THOMAS, a soldier of Lieutenant Colonel Sir Andrew Agnew's Company of the Scots Brigade, [De Schotse Brigade], in Brugge [Bruges] on 13 June 1745. [NRS.GD154.636]

NESBIT, EDWARD, to be transported to France or Flanders on board Michael Thomson's ship from Dysart, Fife, in March 1596. [EBR]

NEWTON, THOMAS, an Ensign who was killed at the Battle of Rijmenant on 31 July 1578. [SLC.118] [BR.ms15662]

NICOLSON, THOMAS, master of the Angel was contracted to carry a cargo of almonds, hides, wool, cloth and skins Burntisland in Fife to 'Campfeir in Flanders' in December 1556, but on return voyage was hit by a storm and attacked by an English ship then took refuge in Crail in Fife. [SACB.168]

NICOLSON, THOMAS, master of the Beaumont of Dunbar from Dunbar, East Lothian, to Dunkirk with a cargo of fish on 25 October 1742. [NRS.E504.10.1]

NISBET, Sir JOHN, with the army in Brugge [Bruges], Gent [Ghent] and Brussels in 1740s. [NRS.GD237.1.106]

NIVEN, JOHN, master of the Fortune of London contracted with Theodore and Philip Jansen, merchants in Angoulesme in France, for shipment of a cargo of brandy, wine and paper to Van Reickhegen a merchant in Oostende but instead went to other ports where he sold the cargo, then sailed to Burntisland in Fife in 1680. [RPCS.VI.520/535]

NIXON, JOSEPH, a soldier of Lieutenant Colonel Sir Andrew Agnew's Company of the Scots Brigade, [De Schotse Brigade], in Brugge [Bruges] on 13 June 1745. [NRS.GD154.636]

NORRIE, ALEXANDER, a Scot, was married in Bergen op Zoom, Brabant, on 3 January 1762. [WBA]

OGILVY, DAVID, with the army in Brugge [Bruges] a letter dated around 1740 from Sir John Ogilvy of Inverquharity, in Angus. [NRS.GD205.25.186]

OGILVY, GEORGE, Provost of Edinburgh, negotiating with the Council of Antwerp concerning a trading agreement, in 1539. [NRS.GD149.264.f135]

OGILVY, JOHN, from Dundee to Flanders on a trading voyage in September 1591, also in November 1597. [DWCB.110]

OGILVIE, WILLIAM, a Captain of Colonel Hepburn's Regiment, was killed in battle at Bergen [Mons] in Vlaanderen [Flanders] in September 1709. [NRS.GD248.18.4; GD77.200.1]

OLIVIERS, NEELTJE, daughter of Bartel Oliviers from Dundee who settled in Veere, was educated in Brugge [Bruges] and married Randolf Sterk in the 1550s. [Veere Court of Chancery]

OSWALD, HENRY, master of the Isobel of Kirkcaldy trading between Kirkcaldy in Fife and Vlaanderen [Flanders] in 1681. [NRS.E72.9.10]

OVERDALE, GERARD, a merchant in Bruges, supplied furniture to Edinburgh in 1481. [ERS.IX.153]

PANTON, Brigadier T., in Gent, [Ghent] a letter dated 13 April 1712 to the Earl of Forfar. [NRAS.2177.5306]

PATERSON, GEORGE, a skipper from Leith to Flanders in 1504. [ATS]

PATERSON, GEORGE, a Scot, waS married in Bergen op Zoom, Brabant, on 23 July 1734. [WA]

PATERSON, HENRY, master of the Martin of South Ferry in Fife from Vlaanderen [Flanders] to Dundee in 1614, 1615, 1616, 1617, and 1618. [DSL]

PATERSON, JOHN, master of the Andrew of Dundee arrived in Aberdeen from Vlaanderen [Flanders] in 1612, [ASW.73]; master of the John of Dundee arrived in Dundee from Vlaanderen [Flanders] in 1613. [DSL]

PATERSON, ROBERT, master of the Andrew of Dundee from Vlaanderen [Flanders] to Aberdeen in 1612. [ASW.73]

PATON, ANDREW ARCHIBALD, in Brussels, son and heir of Andrew Paton a saddler in Edinburgh who died on 13 October 1852. [NRS.S/H.1855]

PATRICK, JOHN, master of the James and Margaret of Dundee trading between Dundee and Dunkirk in 1770. [NRS.E504.11.7]

PAUL, JOHN, and some other embroiderers, from Flanders to Scotland in 1512. [ATS]

PENDRICH, JOHN, a labourer from Aberdeen, was admitted as a burgess of Antwerp in 1537. [AB.398]

PETRIE, ANDREW, master of the Greyhound of Aberdeen trading between Oostende [Ostend] and Aberdeen in 1664. [ASW.515]

PETRIE, ROBERT, master of the Margaret of Montrose from Montrose, Angus, to Oostende [Ostend] in September 1749. [NRS.E504.24.2]

PETIERSOUN, ABRAHAM, from Flanders, was granted the monopoly of mining gold, silver, lead and copper in Scotland for 12 years on 17 February 1577, and on 24 June 1578 he applied to bring in 'gude and sufficient wirkmen for wirking at the said mynis'. [RPCS.III.2]

PHILP, DAVID, master of the Christian of Kirkcaldy trading between Kirkcaldy and Brugge [Bruges] in 1681. [NRS.E72.10/11/12]

PIETERS, CATRIJN, from Antwerp, married John Bartholemew from Aberdeen, in Gouda on 13 May 1590. [Gouda Marriage Register]

PITCAIRN, DAVID, a merchant in Leith trading with Flanders from 1819 until 1820. [NRS.CS96.3525]

POLLOCK, JOHN, a merchant in Edinburgh trading with Oostende [Ostend] in 1784. [NRS.CS96.808]

PREIT, LAURENCE, born in Flanders, a servant of Jacob Mittenete in Bruges, was captured at sea on a Scottish ship and imprisoned in Yarmouth, England, in 1395. [CDS.V.8]

PRENTICE, THOMAS, from Edinburgh, was married in Bergen op Zoom, Brabant, on 21 February 1721. [WBA]

PRESCHO, JAMES, a skipper in Montrose, in Angus, master of the Jean of Montrose trading with Oostende [Ostend] in 1681. [NRS.E72.16.3]

PRESCHOUR, MATTHEW, a merchant and factor in Brugge, [Bruges], Flanders, a deed in 1714. [NRS.RD4.115.945]

PRESTALL, ... is in Flanders, and from thence it is thought he will return to Scotland, 1570'. [CSP.III.59]

PRESTON, Colonel GEORGE, left a legacy in Gent, [Ghent] a letter to the Earl of Mar, dated 12 December 1707. [NRS.GD124.15.730]

PRETTE, JOHN, was bound for Flanders in 1494. [ATS]

PRIDE, ROBERT, mariner, from Leith with a cargo of tobacco bound for Dunkirk on 1 January 1744. [NRS.E504.22.1]

PRINGALL, JOHN, was bound for Flanders in 1494. [ATS]

PRINGLE, Sir JOHN, Physician General to the British Forces in Flanders, letters from 1742 until 1743. [NRS.GD18.5912]

PROSSER, MATTHEW, in Bruges, agent for Isaac Macartney a merchant in Belfast around 1705. [PRONI]

PURDYE, RICHARD, deceased, an employee of the East India Company of Flanders, left a legacy with the Kirk Session of Veere for his wife Agnes Napier and their two children, which the clerk of Edinburgh Town Council collected on 23 August 1638. [EBR]

QUENTIN, JAMES, a Professor at the Royal Military School in Leuven, Brabant, until 1782, later settled in Perth as a teacher of French by 15 October 1787. [NRS.GD359.24.6.130]

QUENSEY, LOUIS, a stamper became a burgess of the Canongait in 1701. [CBR]

RAITT, ROBERT, a skipper in Montrose, Angus, arrived in Aberdeen from Vlaanderen [Flanders] in November 1614. [DSL]

RAMSAY, ALEXANDER, master of the Griffin, a skipper trading between Vlaanderen [Flanders] and Aberdeen in 1599-1612. [ASW.44]

RAMSAY, HENRY, from Dundee, was accused of murdering William Malison in Flanders during 1541. [RPSS.2.4322]

RAMSAY, JAMES, in Brugge, [Bruges], a letter to his brother Sir John Ramsay of Whitehill, dated 1691. [NRS.GD143.69.134]

RAMSAY, Colonel, at Leith aboard ship with army recruits bound for [Vlaanderen] Flanders in 1691. [RPCS.XVI.1.127]

RANKEILLOR, JOHN, master of the Three Brothers of Pool trading between Aberdeen and Duinkerken [Dunkirk] in November 1751, also from Perth and Duinkerken [Dunkirk] in 1753. [NRS.E504.1.4//27.3]

RANKEILLOR, THOMAS, master of the Providence of St Andrews, Fife, trading with Brugge [Bruges] from there to Kirkcaldy in Fife on 13 October 1690. [NRS.E72.9.17]

RANKINE, ROBERT, from Dunkirk to Dundee on 16 August 1682, [DCA.GD.Hu.SF.3/1];99 master of the Hopewell of Dundee trading with Oostende [Ostend] in 1691. [NRS.E72.7.5]

RATTRAY, LACHLAN, a Sergeant in Brigadier Preston's Regiment in Flanders from 1712 until 1717. [NRS.RH4.45]

REDPATH, ANDREW, master of the Angel which transported 35 barrels of salt beef from Ross for the Earl of Morton in 1576. [RPSS.VIII.318]

REID, HENRY, master of the Providence of Perth trading between Perth and Duinkerken [Dunkirk] in 1751 and 1753. [NRS.E504.27.3]

REID, JOHN, the macer, was sent to Leith to arrest some ships recently arrived from Flanders, on 9 December 1571. [Accounts of the Treasurer of Scotland, vol. xii, 1566-1574]

REID, JOHN, a soldier of Lieutenant Colonel Sir Andrew Agnew's Company of the Scots Brigade, [De Schotse Brigade], in Brugge [Bruges] on 13 June 1745. [NRS.GD154.636]

REID, THOMAS and PATRICK, shipped a cargo of wool from Aberdeen aboard the Barbara of Aberdeen, and the 'silver' or money they received was to be sent back to Aberdeen aboard the ship, a court case dated 16 March 1489. [ABR]

REIDIE, DAVID, master of the Dolphin of Burntisland trading between Kirkcaldy in Fife and Oostende [Ostend] between 1669 and 1672. [NRS.E72.9.4/5]

REYNOLDS, GEORGE, a soldier of Lieutenant General James Sinclair's Regiment of Foot, married Jean Connelly, in Brugge [Bruges] on 21 November 1744, a Process of Nullity of Marriage in 1752. [NRS.CC8.6.340]

RICHARDSON, EPHIAS, master of the George of Pittenweem in Fife, arrived in Leith from Oostende [Ostend] with a cargo of madder, yellow wood, lintseed, lint, candy, hops, raisins, tow, hemp, and thread in March 1666. [NRS.E72.15.2]

RICHARDSON, JOHN, a soldier of Lieutenant Colonel Sir Andrew Agnew's Company of the Scots Brigade, [De Schotse Brigade], in Brugge [Bruges] on 13 June 1745. [NRS.GD154.636]

RICHMOND, ADAM, [Adam Ritzmon] a citizen of Antwerpen [Antwerp] around 1540. [SA.Antwerpen Poorterboek]

RIDDER, NICOLAS, master of the Vlaamse Ridder van Oostende [Flemish Knight of Ostend], from Bo'ness, West Lothian, with coal, salt, and sheepskins bound for Ostend on 15 May 1666. [NRS.E72.5.-]

RIKKER, JOSIAS, a gunner in Edinburgh Castle in 1540. [SFP]

RITCHIE, ALEXANDER, master of the Nelly of Leith trading between Duinkerken [Dunkirk] and Perth in 1765. [NRS.E504.27.3]

ROB, ALEXANDER, in Innerpeffray in Perthshire, admitted illicitly trading with Flanders and Danzig him not being a freeman of Perth on 16 September 1552. [Perth Guildry Records]

ROBERT, a Fleming who settled in Upper Lanarkshire before 1200, at a site named Roberton. [SFP.50]

ROBERTSON, or COLLIER, Captain DAVID ALEXANDER, in Bergen op Zoom, Brabant, a deed in 1664. [NRS.GD40.1.141]

ROBERTSON, JAMES, master of the Sophia of Anstruther from Duinkerken [Dunkirk] to Anstruther in Fife in September 1742. [NRS.E504.3.1]

ROBERTSON, JOHN, master of the Morning Star from Oostende [Ostend] to Leith with a cargo of almonds, currants and paper, in 1665. [NRS.E72.15.2]

ROBERTSON, WALTER, a merchant and treasurer of Aberdeen, was sent to Brugge [Bruges] to purchase a replacement ensign for the burgh, on 3 April 1616. [ABR]

ROBERTSON, WILLIAM, a merchant in Brussels, a bankrupt in 1792-1793. [NRS.NRAS.3955.60.3.16]

ROCHEID, JAMES, a merchant and baillie of Leith, and his partner Robert Trotter, shipped a cargo of salmon via Berwick bound for Neiwpoort in West Flanders, where it was confiscated by Alpherus Diksoun before 1 January 1645. [EBR]

RODDART, CORNELIUS, master of the St Philip van Oostende [Ostend] trading between Oostende and Kirkcaldy in Fife in August 1670. [NRS.E72.9.]

ROGER, ANDREW, master of the Margaret from Ostend to Bo'ness, West Lothian, with a cargo of madder, brazilwood, hemp, whale bones, ginger, raisins, candy, hemp, sweet oil, blue stain, tow and cloth, in 1690. [NRS.E72.5.-]

ROLLOCK, THOMAS, master of the Helen of Dundee, from Duinkerken [Dunkirk] to Dundee in January 1685. [NRS.E72.7.14]

ROLLOSS, VOLKART, a harpooner aboard the Dundee of Dundee, arrived in Dundee on 25 July 1753, also in 1754. from Greenland. [NRS.E508.51.8]

ROSS, CHARLES, a Lieutenant General of Queen Anne's Forces in Flanders around 1760, a sasine, [NRS.RS37.XI.506]

ROSS, DAVID, a Scot, was married in Bergen op Zoom, Brabant, on 26 October 1698. [WBA]

ROSS, JAMES, in Brussels imported Spey salmon from Thomas Bannerman in Aberdeen, around 1782. [NRS.GD44.43.267]

ROSS, JOHN, born 1762 in Kincardine, Easter Ross, enlisted on 25 June 1804, a private soldier of the 2nd Battalion of the 78th Foot, stationed at Nieuport in Flanders, and was discharged on 6 May 1816. [TNA.WO.97/889/135]

ROSS, ROBERT, master of the Buxton of Dundee trading between Perth and Duinkerken [Dunkirk] in 1749. [NRS.E504.27.1]

ROW, Colonel ARCHIBALD, in Breda, Brabant, a letter dated 1702. [NRS.GD24.5.221]; his Regiment of Foot was bound to Flanders in 1702. [NRS.E.94.107]

RUGY, HENRY, master of the Gabriel of Leith sailed from Leith with a cargo bound for the market at Brugge [Bruges] in June 1514, the ship was moored at Vlissingen [Flushing] overnight awaiting the tide but was stolen and sold to Englishmen. A letter to Anna of Veere on 29 September 1517. [LJV.52]

RUSSELL, ANDREW, a Scottish merchant based in Rotterdam, trading with Antwerp and Gent in 1680. [NRS.RH15.100.387]

RUTHERFORD, ANDREW, a Lieutenant General of the French Army, who had fought in Flanders, France, Germany and Italy, was created Lord Rutherford on 9 January 1661. [RGS.XI.32]

RUTHERFORD, JOHN, a soldier of Lieutenant Colonel Sir Andrew Agnew's Company of the Scots Brigade, [De Schotse Brigade], in Brugge [Bruges] on 13 June 1745. [NRS.GD154.636]

RUTHVEN, DOUGALL, a soldier of Lieutenant Colonel Sir Andrew Agnew's Company of the Scots Brigade, [De Schotse Brigade], in Brugge [Bruges] on 13 June 1745. [NRS.GD154.636]

RYMBERS, JACOB, a harpooner aboard the Peggy of Glasgow, arrived in Bo'ness in West Lothian on 1 October 1751 from Greenland. [NRS.E508.48.8]

SABLE, JEAN, master of the privateer Holy Trinity of Oostende, [Ostend] was captured by Captain Robert Gordon and sold in Leith on 17 August 1704. [NRS.AC7.12/130; AC9.130]

SALMOND, ROBERT, a merchant in Perth trading in 'Flisching' [Flushing] in 1545. [Perth Guildry Records]

SANDIS ROBERT, was imprisoned in Flanders, versus James Barton his master, dated September 1557. [ACB.2]

SANDISON, ALEXANDER, born in Scotland a soldier in Flanders, later a cavalry officer in Poland, settled in Ireland, died in Desertcreat, County Tyrone, in 1633. [Church of Ireland, Desetcrest gravestone]

SANGLEIR, CHARLES, a Fleming, versus John Cant a skipper in Leith, in the Admiralty Court in Edinburgh in February 1558. [ACB.87/100/119]

SARNHOLT, NICHOLAS, from Lubeck, petitioned Aberdeen Council, on 2 January 1445, on behalf of a group of German merchants based in Bruges that their ship laden with merchandise had been captured by pirates who sold the stock in Aberdeen. [AGC]

SCHETZ, ERASMUS, possibly a Fleming, was permitted by King James V to prospect for and extract minerals in Scotland in 1527. [RPCS]

SCHORWOOD, ROBERT, master of the Swallow [Zwaluw] from Dundee bound for Vlaanderen [Flanders] in January 1596. [WCB.71]

SCOTT, ALEXANDER, a skipper trading between Nieuwpoort in Vlaanderen [Flanders] and Riga in 1576, and from Brugge [Bruges] and Danzig [Gdansk] in 1578. [RAK/STR]

SCOTT, CORNELIUS, a citizen of Antwerp, a descendant of William Douglas a Scottish Ambassador to Charlesmagne, a birth brief granted by King James VI in Edinburgh on 16 May 1621, which was confirmed at the request of the Count of St Peter Yettensis, baron of Rimiere, Lord of Kinshot and a knight of the Order of St James, on 31 December 1660. [RGS.XI.31]

SCOTT, DAVID, in Antwerp, son of Johanna, daughter of Robert ..., was appointed as her agent for the sale of property in Aberdour, Fife, in a deed dated 16 February 1533. [NRS.GD130.647]

SCOTT, FRANCIS, a letter to his brother in law Charles Baillie from Brussels on 30 August 1828. [NRS.GD157.2561]

SCOTT, GEORGE, a soldier, was granted a pass to travel to Bergen on Zoom in 1628. [TNA,E157,14]

SCOTT, GEORGE, a Captain of the Scottish Army in Belgium, son of James Scot of Lochhill and Anna Scott, daughter of William Scott, a genealogy dated 6 December 1777. [NRS.Lyon Office.G1.228]

SCOTT, JAMES, master of the <u>Christian of Kirkcaldy</u> trading between Brugge [Bruges] and Kirkcaldy in 1670. [NRS.E72.9.4]

SCOTT, JAMES, the younger, master of the <u>Janet of Montrose</u> from Montrose in Angus, to Duinkerken [Dunkirk] in July 1681. [NRS.E72.16.7]

SCOTT, JAMES, in Breda, Brabant, a bill of exchange dated 1748. [NRS.GD45.18.949]

SCOTT, JOHN, in Brussels, letters to Lord Polwarth from 1716 until 1722. [NRS.GD158.1968]

SCOTT, JOHN, master of the <u>Drummond of Greenock</u> trading with Dunkirk in 1769. [NRS.E504.15.17]

SCOTT, LUDOVIC, a Scot, was married in Bergen op Zoom, Brabant, on 16 October 1733. [WBA]

SCOTT, PETER, a citizen of Antwerp, a descendant of William Douglas a Scottish ambassador to Charlesmagne, a birth brief granted by King James VI in Edinburgh on 16 May 1621, which was confirmed at the request of the Count of St Peter Yettensis, baron of Rimiere, Lord of Kinshot and a knight of the Order of St James, on 31 December 1660. [RGS.XI.31]

SCOTT, WILLIAM, master of the James of Burntisland trading between Oostende [Ostend] and Kirkcaldy in 1672. [NRS.E72.9.5]

SCOTT, WILLIAM, a Scot, was married in Bergen op Zoom, Brabant, on 13 March 1685. [WBA]

SCOTT and HAMILTON, merchants in Antwerpen [Antwerp] in 1820. [NRS.CS44.115.76]

SCRYMGEOUR, DAVID, a merchant trading with Antwerpen [Antwerp] between 1678 and 1693. [NRS.CS96.2015]

SCRYMGEOUR, JAMES, a Royal clerk was sent by King James V to Flanders on royal business on 20 September 1532. [LJV.229]

SEATON, GILBERT, born 1606, a soldier who was granted a pass to travel to Antwerpen [Antwerp] in 1632. [TNA.E157.6]

SEATON, LACHLAN, a Sergeant of the Scots Foot Guards in Vlaanderen [Flanders] a deed dated 1695. [NRS.RD4.77.261]

SEGATT, ALEXANDER, formerly in the Canongait, thereafter in Edinburgh, was bound for Flanders in February 1596. [EBR]

SEMPILL, JAMES, a soldier of Lieutenant Colonel Sir Andrew Agnew's Company of the Scots Brigade, [De Schotse Brigade], in Brugge [Bruges] on 13 June 1745. [NRS.GD154.636]

SEMPLE, Lord, bound for Flanders, a letter from his nephew Andrew Semple of Bruntshiels, dated 16 March 1611. [NRS.GD3.5.28]

SETON, LAUCHLAN, a Sergeant of the Scots Regiment of Foot Guards, in Flanders, a deed dated 1694. [NRS.RD4.74.917]

SHAIRP, Captain WALTER, was instructed by John Dalziel to embark, with other officers, on the Nonesuch in Oostende [Ostend] bound for Scotland, in a letter dated 9 November 1696. [NRS.GD30.2093]; a Captain of the Scots Fusiliers, a deed of factory in 1697, [NRS.GD30.461]; a Colonel by 1709, husband of Janet Dalziel. [NRS.GD30.780]

SHAIRP, Colonel WILLIAM, at camp near Lille, a letter dated 5 September 1708. [NRS.GD30.1755]

SHARP, DUNCAN, from Campbeltown in Argyll, married Janet Ferguson from Yperen in Flanders in the Scots Kirk in Rotterdam on 12 February 1774. [GAR]

SHEARER, [SCHERAR] WILLIAM, in Aberdeen, trading with Lankyn West, a merchant in Brugge [Bruges] on 26 January 1433, a dispute re wine. [ABR]

SHEPHERD, GEORGE, master of the Christian of Perth trading between Perth and Duinkerken [Dunkirk] in 1749. [NRS.E504.24.1]

SIBBALD, JOHN, a Scot, was married in Bergen op Zoom, Brabant, on 25 September 1733. [WBA]

SIBBALD, PETER, a Scot, was married in Bergen op Zoom, Brabant, on 12 January 1702. [WBA]

SIME, JAMES, master of the brig Aurora of Dundee, when bound from Riga in Latvia for Lisbon in Portugal, was captured by Captain Blankman of the privateer Ancreon van Duinkerken [Ancreon of Dunkirk] on 23 December 1798 and taken to Bergen in Norway. [AJ.2665]

SIMMERS, ALEXANDER, in Kales [Calais] a letter to the Duke of Hamilton, dated 1712. [NRS.GD406.1.5815]

SIMPSON, ALEXANDER, master of the Katherine of Kirkcaldy trading between Brugge [Bruges] and Kirkcaldy in 1683. [NRS.E72.9.14]

SIMSON, ROBERT, in Brugge, [Bruges], was granted land in Edinburgh by Richard Simson a skinner burgess, on 29 March 1576. [NRS.GD1.533.455]

SIMPSON, THOMAS, master of the Margaret of Dundee which was captured off Buchan Ness by the privateer Anacreon van Duinkerken, Captain Blankman, on 19 December 1798. [AJ.2665]

SINCLAIR, JAMES, a letter dated Lille on 21 June 1784, to Alexander Bower of Kingoldrum concerning his children at Douie. [NRS.GD53.149]

SINCLAIR, Captain JAMES, of the 79th Regiment, in Ghent bound for Brussels a latter to his sister Betsy Sinclair in Thurso in Caithness, dated 28 May 1815. [NRS.GD139.369]

SINCLAIR, Captain JOHN, in Brugge [Bruges] a letter dated 1 December 1696 from the Earl of Orkney. [NRS.GD154.636]

SINCLAIR, JOHN, in Gent, [Ghent] a letter to the Duke of Hamilton, dated 25 October 1712. [NRS.GD406.1.5814]

SINCLAIR, JOHN, a Captain of the 79th Regiment, on the march from Gent [Ghent] to Brussel in 1815, a letter dated 28 May 1815, he was killed at the Battle of Waterloo. [NRS.GD139.369]

SKENE, FRANCIS, in Gent, [Ghent], a letter to his uncle Captain John Skene in Edinburgh, dated 30 January 1712. [NRS.NRAS.897.118]

SKINNER, DAVID, master of the Eagle of Montrose trading with Oostende [Ostend] in 1744. [NRS.E504.24.

SLEVMAN, JOHN, a waulker [fuller] in Dunfermline, Fife, in 1499. [DBR]

SMEATON, ANDREW, master of the Post of Dundee bound from Dundee to Duinkerken [Dunkirk] in March 1686. [NRS.E72.7.24]

SMITH, ANDREW, a Lieutenant of Colonel Stewart's Regiment in Flanders, [Vlaanderen], testament confirmed with the Commissariat of Edinburgh on 28 July 1749. [NRS]

SMITH, DAVID, master of the David arrived in Dundee in March 1613 from Vlaanderen [Flanders]. [DSL]

SMITH, DAVID, a skipper in Montrose, Angus, master of the Elizabeth of Montrose trading with Duinkerken [Dunkirk] in 1681. [NRS.E72.16.10]

SMITH, HENRY, a Scot, was married in Bergen op Zoom, Brabant, on 17 November 1633. [WBA]

SMITH, JOHN, a mariner burgess of Dundee, master of the Elspeth arrived in Dundee from Vlaanderen [Flanders] in July 1613 and in May 1614. [DSL]

SMYTH, Ensign PATRICK in Gent, [Ghent], brother of David Smyth of Methven, a letter describing the voyage from Leith to Gent [Ghent] and the attack by four French warships, dated 17 April 1709. [NRS.GD190.1.27]; was planning to leave Brussels, a letter dated 25 December 1709. [NRS.GD190.1.30]

SNOWDEN, a herald, was bound for Flanders in 1494. [ATS]

SOCHAN, PIETER, a gunsmith in Edinburgh around 1680.[SFP]

SPENCE, JAMES, a soldier of Lieutenant Colonel Sir Andrew Agnew's Company of the Scots Brigade, [De Schotse Brigade], in Brugge [Bruges] on 13 June 1745. [NRS.GD154.636]

STEEN, JOHN, a Scot, was married in Bergen op Zoom, Brabant, on 31 March 1637. [WBA]

STERCK, GERALD, possibly a Fleming, was permitted by King James V to prosect and extract minerals in Scotland in 1527. [RPCS]

STEVENSON, JAMES, a thief, possibly from Paisley, imprisoned in Edinburgh Tolbooth, was sent to Flanders or Holland as a soldier under Captain Thomas Hamilton on 1 April 1684. [ETR.28.3.1684]; [RPCS.3.8.691]

STEWART, ALEXANDER, a letter from Oostende or Ghent re French Artillery officers, dated 6 January 1794. [NRS.NRAS.3955.60.1.409]

STEWART, CATHERINE RAMSAY, wife of Fergus Ferguson, late of Small's Wynd, Dundee, died at English Noon Street, 1 St Peter's Street, Ghent, on 16 July 1865. [PJD.403]

STEWART, C. W., in Bergen op Zoom, Brabant, a letter dated 1732. [NRS.CD1.407.24]

STEWART, JAMES, a merchant in Inverness, trading with Brugge [Bruges] between 1716 and 1718.

STEWART, JAMES, born 1785, a weaver from Hamilton, Lanarkshire, enlisted in the 2nd Battalion of the 78th Regiment of Foot in 1804, a Sergeant by 1826, served in Holland and Flanders and fought at the Battle of Mereexem. [H78.125]

STEWART, JOHN, [Jan Stavaert], a citizen of Antwerpen [Antwerp] around 1540. [SA.Antwerpen Poorterboek]

STEWART, JOHN, from Aberdeen, then in Vlaanderen [Flanders], expected to return on 10 July 1540. [ACR.810]

STEWART, WILLIAM, the Albany Herald, was sent to Norway, Denmark and Flanders in 1567. [Accounts of the Treasurer of Scotland, vol.xii, 75, 1566-1574]

STEWART, Sir WILLIAM, Commendator of Pittenweem, claimed for services in Flanders and Brabant, before 1588. [CSP.Foreign.September 1588]

STEWART, Colonel, from Pittenweem, was granted 'letters of mark' [authorised privateer], see letters from the authorities of the Low Countries, 1589. [EBR]

STEWART, Sir WILLIAM, of Houston, the Scottish Ambassador to Flanders in 1594. [NRS.GD30.17]

STIRLING, ALEXANDER, of Achyle, formerly a Lieutenant of the Earl of Tullibardine's Regiment in Vlaanderen [Flanders[a soldier who died at Darien in Panama in 1699, testament confirmed with the Commissariat of Edinburgh in 1707. [NRS]

STIRLING, JOHN, in Kortrijk, [Courtrai], a letter to his uncle George Stirling re army and friends in Vlaanderen [Flanders], dated 22 November 1646. [NRS.GD24.2.5.4]

STIRLING, WILLIAM, later Sir William Stirling of Ardoch, an Ensign in Captain Patrick Graham's Company of Colyear's Regiment, at Yperen [Ypres] in 1750, a Lieutenant in 1754. [NRS.GD23.6.53; GD24.1.455]

STIRLING, WILLIAM MORAY, of Abercairny, was wounded at the Battle of Waterloo in 1815, two letters. [NRS.GD24.1.512]

STOBB, WILLIAM, a mariner from Perth, imprisoned in Duinkerken [Dunkirk] awaiting ransom for him, the ship and cargo captured by a French privateer when voyaging from Gothenborg in Sweden to Perth, in late eighteenth century. [NRS.B59.37.13.51]

STOTT, JAMES, master of the Christian of Kirkcaldy from Brugge [Bruges] to Kirkcaldy in Fife with a cargo of tow and lint on 4 May 1670. [NRS.E29.9]

STRACHAN, JAMES, master of the James of Dundee trading with Flanders in 1616-1617. [DSL]

STRACHAN, JAMES, master of the James of Dundee from Vlaanderen [Flanders] to Dundee in October 1616 and October 1617. [DSL]

STRACHAN, Captain JOHN, was permitted to recruit 100 men as soldiers for the Low Countries of Flanders on 2 June 1596. [EBR]; son of Thomas Strachan and his wife Helen Scott in Forgan in Fife, died in Flanders before September 1600. [MSC.II.54]

STRACHAN, WILLIAM, a skipper from Leven in Fife, from Vlaanderen [Flanders] to Aberdeen in 1637. [ASW.214]

STRATH, THOMAS, a Scot, was married in Bergen op Zoom, Brabant, on 18 July 1736. [WBA]

STRATHNAVAR, Colonel Lord, his Regiment of Foot was bound for Flanders in April 1694, and returned in April 1699, vouchers. [NRS.E94.14/64]

STRONACH, JAMES, a skipper in Dundee, from Vlaanderen [Flanders] to Aberdeen in 1636. [ASW.213]

STUART, Prince DAVID, fought at the Battle of Buirenfoss in French Flanders, with the French against the English.

STUART, King JAMES II, marriage documents with Marie de Gueldres, dated between 1448 and 1450. [NRS.RH1.2.983.3]

STUART, King JAMES V, letters of accreditation by Emperor Charles V regarding his chamberlain Pierre, Sieur de Bozubay and the Burgandy King of Arms, sent on a mission to Scotland on 14 January 1532. [NRS.SP9l3]; letters with the burgomaster of Antwerp, dated 14 December 1532. [NRS.GD249.2.2.1/f72]; a letter to the Council and Senate of Antwerp proposing that Scottish merchants leave to port of Antwerp in 1540. [NRS.GD149.264.f146]; a letter to the Council and Senate of Antwerp asking if the assets of a dead Scottish merchant be paid to his relatives, in 1540. [NRS.GD149..F147/255]

STUART, JOHN, later the Earl of Traquair, in Brugge, [Bruges], letters from 1759 until 1761. [NRS.NRAS.3466.110.2-14]

STUART, LUCY, in Brugge, [Bruges] a letter to Mary, the Dowager Countess of Traquair, dated 16 June 1758. [NRAS.3666.14.2]

STUPART, DAVID, a soldier of Lieutenant Colonel Sir Andrew Agnew's Company of the Scots Brigade, [De Schotse Brigade], in Brugge [Bruges] on 13 June 1745. [NRS.GD154.636]

SUTHERLAND, ALEXANDER, a soldier of Lieutenant Colonel Sir Andrew Agnew's Company of the Scots Brigade, [De Schotse Brigade], in Brugge [Bruges] on 13 June 1745. [NRS.GD154.636]

SUTHERLAND, HUGH, a Captain in General Murray's Regiment in Flanders a deed dated 1714. [NRS.RD2.103/2.636]

SWARD, MATTHEW, master of the Isobel of Kirkcaldy from Brugge [Bruges] to Kirkcaldy in May 1670. [NRS.E72.9]

SWINTON, GILBERT, a Scot, was married in Bergen op Zoom, Brabant, on 27 December 1634. [WBA]

SWINTON, JAMES, son of Sir John Swinton of Mersington, a Lieutenant of Colonel Lauder's Regiment in Vlaanderen [Flanders] in 1707. [NRS.AC8.87]

SWINTON, Sir JOHN, a Scottish merchant in London, trading with Oostende [Ostend] between 1673 and 1677. [NRS.CS96.3264]

SWITINOIS, Captain, master of the Myrmidon of Dunkirk, which was sold in Leith on 12 August 1704. [NRS.AC7.11] [NRS.AC9.59]

SYMMER, ……., in Ghent, Flanders, a letter dated 1712. [NRS.GD406.71.5856]

TANCRED, a Fleming who settled in Upper Lanarkshire before 1200, at a site named Thankerton. [SFP.50]

TANNEKEN, N., from Ghent, in Flanders, married John Robertson from Edinburgh, in Rotterdam on 10 July 1588. [GAR]

TANNER, ….., a seaman aboard the whaler Raith of Leith when returning from Greenland was captured by a French privateer off the Shetland Island and imprisoned in Dunkirk in 1794. [PL.296]

TAYLOR, PETER, a merchant in Perthshire, admitted illicitly trading with Flanders and Danzig him not being a freeman of Perth on 16 September 1552. [Perth Guildry Records]

TENNANT, WILLIAM, master of the Anna of Leith returned to Leith on 3 October 1681 from Oostende [Ostend]. [NRS.E72.15.23]

THOMAS, THOMAS, a citizenof Antwerp around 1540. [SA.Antwerpen Poorterboek]

THOMSON, DAVID, a Scot, was married in Bergen op Zoom, Brabant, on 16 March 1655. [WBA]

THOMSON, JAMES, a soldier who was granted a pass to travel to Vlaanderen [Flanders] on 6 June 1631. [TNA.E157.5]

THOMSON, JAMES, master of the Providence of Montrose from Montrose in Angus to Dunkirk in September 1748. [NRS.E504.24.2]

THOMPSON, JOHN, a Scot, was married in Bergen op Zoom, Brabant, on 3 November 1621. [WBA]

THOMSON, ROBERT, a Scot, was married in Bergen op Zoom, Brabant, on 3 November 1621. [WBA]

THOMSON, THOMAS, a citizen of Antwerp around 1540. [SA.Antwerpen, Poorterboek]

THOMSON, WILLIAM, a Canon of the Church of Our Lady at Antwerpen [Antwerp], was sent to Edinburgh to persuade the Scots to establish Antwerpen [Antwerp] as their Staple Port in the Low Countries in 1539. He replaced Alexander Fotheringam, deceased, at St Ninian's there. [SSN.54][PSS.2.2722]

THOMPSON, WILLIAM, a Scot, was married in Bergen op Zoom, Brabant, on 23 March 1707. [WBA]

THORNTON, GODFREY, in Brussel, letters to Ensign Erskine of the 1st Guards Regiment, dated 1814 to 1815. [NRS.GD24.15.1740]

THORNTON, JOHN, a soldier of Lieutenant Colonel Sir Andrew Agnew's Company of the Scots Brigade, [De Schotse Brigade],in Brugge [Bruges] on 13 June 1745. [NRS.GD154.636]

TODD, GEORGE, a merchant from Edinburgh, who was admitted as a burgess of Antwerpen [Antwerp] in 1545. [Antwerpen Poorterboek]

TODD, GEORGE, master of the John of Kirkcaldy trading between Brugge [Bruges] and Kirkcaldy in 1681. [NRS.E72.9.12]

TOURS, CLEMENT, a glass-wright in Edinburgh in 1616. [SFP.66]

TOYKER, GABRIEL, a webster [weaver], was admitted as a burgess and guilds-brother of Perth on 18 September 1552. [PGB]

TULLOCH, HUBERT, a Scot, was married in Bergen op Zoom, Brabant, on 19 October 1768. [WBA]

TYNDALL, ONESIPHORUS, journals of the Grand Tour of Europe from 1813 until 1816, including Flanders. [NRS.GD152.92.1]

TYTLER, CHARLES, from Midmar in Aberdeenshire, and Elizabeth Miller from Hertenbosch in Brabant, were married in the Scots Kirk in Rotterdam on 30 January 1740. [GAR]

VAN BOBAERT, CURTUS, and Geraldus Timmerman, merchants of Danzig, residing in Antwerp, received a letter from the Council of Antwerp, which was forwarded to Henricus Beyer, a merchant of Danzig, residing in Hull, Yorkshire, regarding a ship of Amsterdam which was bound for Danzig but was taken to Scotland, dated 30 October 1563. [NRS.RH9.5.19]

VAN BRONCKHURST, ARNOLD, a Flemish painter at the Court of King James VI [IPR] [SFP.64]

VAN BRUCK, JAN, master of the Yung Dochter van Brugge [Young Daughter of Bruges] arrived in Aberdeen in 1665. [ASW.525]

VAN DER HEILL, JEREMY, a dyer in St Paul's Work, Canongait, from 1621. [BOEC.XVIII.58]

VAN DER HEIDEN ......, in Scotland in 1708. [NRS.AC8.97]

VAN DER STAEL, CECILIA, relict of John Newton of that Ilk, a marriage contract recorded 7 May 1669. [NRS.RD4.23.696]

VAN RATEN, PHILIPE, was born in Brugge [Bruges], but recently lived in England, wished to become naturalised in Scotland, then establish a woollen mill in Kelso, in Roxburghshire, petitioned the Scottish Privy Council in February 1672, [RPCS.III.472]; a merchant in Brugge [Bruges] from 1674-1675, [NRS.RD4.34.453; RD2.37.383/692; RD3.38.119]; a merchant from Brugge, [Bruges], was admitted as a burgess of Edinburgh in 1684. [EBR][SFP.65]

VAN DOENGHEN, GERTRUDE, relict of George Douglas a routmaster, a bond recorded 26 August 1661. [NRS.RD4.3.154]

VAN GENT, FRANCIS, a linen stamper in Edinburgh, a receipt dated 13 March 1691, [NRS.GD112,9.47]; a decreet dated 1693, [NRS.CS138.681]; a burgess of the Canongait, Edinburgh, in 1702. [CBR][SFP.66]

VAN HAELEMIS, MAYCHEN, from Flanders, married Alexander Mabon, from Edinburgh, a sword burnisher in Gorkum, South Holland, in Leiden on 28 January 1605. [Leiden Marriage Register]

VAN HEASTEIN, LEONARD, a trumpeter to Lord Newbattle's troop, a deed, 1691. [NRS.RD4.67.841]

VAN HEGGIN, FRANCIS, an engraver, was admitted as a Freeman of the Hammermen of the Canongait in 1669; his son, a gunsmith, became a burgess on his marriage to the daughter of a burgess. [BOEC.XIX.30]

VAN HETTINGA, AURELIA CATHERINA, spouse of Sir Robert Hamilton of Silvertounhill, a deed 1691. [NRS.RD2.73.119]

VAN MASTRICH, PHILIP, master of the Heilige Michael van Oostende, [Holy Michael of Ostend], from Bo'ness in West Lothian with a cargo of coal bound for Vlaanderen [Flanders] in August 1666. [NRS.E72.5]

VAN MOORSELL, THEODOR, from Antwerpen [Antwerp], was admitted as a burgess and guilds-brother of Glasgow on 27 July 1786. [GBR]

VAN NUFFEEL, JAN, in Brussels, a letter from Grant Crawford in Amsterdam dated 26 April 1739. [NRS.GD110.1112]

VAN REICKKHEGEN, ..., a merchant in Ostend in 1680. [RPCS.VI.520/535]

VAN PASSEL, JOANNE MARIE, in Gent, [Ghent], a letter to Sir William Dick of Prestonfield, dated 5 April 1734. [NRS.RH15.36.93A]

VAN SLUYR, ALBERTUS, master of the St Helena van Oostende [St Helen of Bruges], arrived in Bo'ness, West Lothian with a cargo of madder, French wine, tobacco, lint, soap, sugar, lead, yellow wood, raisons, brissalls and gingerbread in May 1667. [NRS.E72.5.-]

VAN SOUN, ABRAHAM, a goldsmith from Vlaanderen [Flanders], a naturalised Scot and husband of Janet, daughter of Alexander Gilbert a goldsmith burgess, was admitted as a burgess of Edinburgh on 17 February 1587. [EBR] [SFP.64]

VAN SOUN, ADRIAN, a painter at the Court of King James VI, father of Adam de Colone who was born in Scotland but went to Vlaanderen [Flanders] 'To improve his art'. [RPCS.XIII.698]

VAN SOUN, MARION, residing in Kirkcaldy, Fife, in 1584. [EUL.LC.1073]

VAN STRAETEN, PHILIPE, a merchant from Bruges [Brugge], was admitted as a burgess and guilds-brother [a member of the Merchants Guild] of Edinburgh in 1684. [EBR]

VAN WEERT, JOHANNES HENDRICK, a deed of factory and commission, 14 January 1671. [NRS]; was married in Bergen op Zoom, Brabant, on 28 September 1714. [WBA]

VEITCH SAMUEL, born 9 December 1668 in Edinburgh. A student at Utrecht, Later, as an officer of the Royal Scots Dragoons he fought in Vlaanderen [Flanders], in 1698 he took part in the Darien Expedition from there to New York, a merchant in Albany and Boston, he participated in the attack on Port Royal, Acadia, Governor of Nova Scotia from1710 until 1717, died in London in 1732. [SCS] [NEHGS] [UU]

VER ANDER, ARIAN, master of the St Jan van Brugge [St John of Bruges] from Kirkcaldy, Fife, with coal bound for Brugge [Bruges] on 6 April 1681. [NRS.E72.9.10]

VER HAGAN, FRANCIS, a bookseller and burgess of the Canongait, residing in Coutts Court. [CBR]

VERNER, JACK, a merchant, and his son and heir Patrick Vernor a burgess of Edinburgh, assignees of Hans Hermanson, a merchant in Antwerp, also Adrian Harmanson, a merchant in Middelburg, versus John Robertson, son of Thomas Robertson, a burgess of Montrose in Angus, 8 December 1592.

VETCH, WILLIAM, formerly a Lieutenant of the Earl of Angus's Regiment in Vlaanderen [Flanders], later in Darien, Panama, died aboard the Hope in 1699, testament confirmed with the Commissariat of Edinburgh in 1707. [NRS]

VYSER, THOMAS CLAASE, a harpooner aboard the Peggy of Glasgow, arrived in Bo'ness in West Lothian on 1 October 1751 from Greenland. [NRS.E508.48.8]

WADE, JAMES, a soldier of Lieutenant Colonel Sir Andrew Agnew's Company of the Scots Brigade, [De Schotse Brigade], in Brugge [Bruges] on 13 June 1745. [NRS.GD154.636]

WALKER, ARCHIBALD, a soldier of Lieutenant Colonel Sir Andrew Agnew's Company of the Scots Brigade, [De Schotse Brigade], in Brugge [Bruges] on 13 June 1745. [NRS.GD154.636]

WALKER, WILLIAM, a skipper of Fittie, Aberdeen, trading with Vlaanderen [Flanders] in 1628/1633/1637 [ASW.155/182/223/225/232/241/248/278]

WALLACE, ROBERT, a soldier of Lieutenant Colonel Sir Andrew Agnew's Company of the Scots Brigade, [De Schotse Brigade], in Brugge [Bruges] on 13 June 1745. [NRS.GD154.636]

WALLINC, WILLEM, [alias William Wallange] master of the Guild of Painters in Brugge [Bruges] around 1506, from 1505 until 1516 was in the service of the Bishop of Dunkeld and the Bishop of Aberdeen. [PS97]

WALLS, THOMAS, a merchant in Antwerp, witness to a charter by James Maitland, son and heir of William Maitland, secretary to Mary, Queen of Scots, in Antwerp on 15 May 1613. [RGS.VII.897]

WARBECK, PERKIN, was born in Kortrijk [Tournai], employed by a Breton merchant in Ireland in 1491, settled in Scotland where he married Lady Catherine Gordon in 1496. [PL56]

WATSON, JAMES, a Scottish burgess of Brugge [Bruges] in 1540. [SSN.56]

WATSON, JOHN, master of the John and Elizabeth of Perth trading between Perth and Duinkerken [Dunkirk] from 1749 until 1750. [NRS.E504.27.1.3]

WATTS, ALLAN, master of the Morton of Aberdour from Kirkcaldy in Fife with a cargo of coal bound for Brugge [Bruges] on 10 March 1681. [NRS.E72.9.10]

WATT, JOHN, of Denmiln, a merchant in Dundee, trading with Antwerp from 1824 until 1829. [NRS.CS96.1329]

WATT, PETER, a Scot, was married in Bergen op Zoom, Brabant, on 20 December 1684. [WBA]

WATTS, WILLIAM, a merchant in Dublin, freighted the St Francis van Antwerpen [St Francis of Antwerp] to sail from Oostende [Ostend] via Dublin bound for Scotland, which was shipwrecked near Portpatrick in Wigtownshire, Scotland in 1666. [NRS.RH9.5.31]

WATT, WILLIAM, a Scot, was married in Bergen op Zoom, Brabant, on 26 December 1732. [WBA]

WATT, WILLIAM, a Lieutenant of the Foot Guards in Vlaanderen [Flanders], deeds dated 1692. [NRS.RD4.70.356/563]

WAUGH, JAMES, from Scotland, married Maycken Gillesdaghter, from Westinde near Nieuwpoort in Flanders, in Leiden in Holland on 25 February 1589. [Leiden Marriage Register]

WAUGH, JAMES, the town piper of Musselburgh, Mid Lothian, was involuntarily taken with a regiment of soldiers aboard a ship in Leith bound for Flanders, The Privy Council ordered his release on 17 February 1691. [RPCS.XVI.I.126] a recruit for the army in Vlaanderen [Flanders], to be put ashore and imprisoned in Canongait Tolbooth, by order of the Privy Council in 1691. [RPCS.XVI.1.127]

WEIR, GEORGE, a Captain of Buchan's Regiment in Flanders, his testament was confirmed on 27 July 1703 with the Commissariat of Edinburgh. [NRS]

WEMYSS, JAMES, a Scot, was married in Bergen op Zoom, Brabant, on 29 May 1621. [WBA]

WEMYSS, ..., at the Battle of Rijmenant in 1578. [BR.ms 15662/10]

WEST, LANKYN, a merchant in Brugge [Bruges] trading with William Shearer in Aberdeen, 26 January 1433. [ABR]

WHITE, ROBERT, master of the Thomas of Kirkcaldy trading between Oostende [Ostend] and Kirkcaldy in Fife, during 1681. [NRS.E72.9.10]

WIISS, PIETER, from Niewport in Flanders, in Aberdeen in 1453. [AGC]

WILLIAM, JACOB, master of the Ewauld of Hamburg formerly a Leith ship which had been captured by a Dunkirk man o' war was retaken by Captain James Binning master of the Gift of God of St Monance, in Fife, off the coast of Norway in May 1628 when bound for Duinkerken [Dunkirk]. [NRS.AV7.1.212]

WILLIAM son of Freskin, was granted the lands of Stratbrok, Duffus, and other, around 1170. [SFP]

WILLIAMSON, JOHN, a Scottish soldier, married Tarijn Jans from Oudenaarde in Flanders, in Leiden on 20 January 1601. [Leiden Marriage Register]

WILLIAMSON, JOHN, master of the Marie of Pittenweem, Fife, trading with Brugge [Bruges] on 13 March 1684. [NRS.E72.9.27]

WILSON, JOHN, a soldier of Lieutenant Colonel Sir Andrew Agnew's Company of the Scots Brigade, [De Schotse Brigade], in Brugge [Bruges] on 13 June 1745. [NRS.GD154.636]

WILSON, THOMAS, master of the John of Leith from Vlaanderen [Flanders] to Leith in September 1631. [SJC.1.197]

WINRAM, GEORGE, of Libertoun, aboard the Elizabeth of Kirkcaldy at Briel in 1649, a letter for the Conservator of the Scots Privileges. [JTC.191]

WINTOUN, ROBERT, servant to James Cunningham a farmer in Waughtoun, aboard ship in Leith, a recruit for the army in Vlaanderen [Flanders], to be out ashore and imprisoned in Canongait Tolbooth, by order of the Privy Council in 1691. [RPCS.XVI.1.127]

WISHART, DANIEL, a mariner aboard the George of Leith was imprisoned in Duinkerken [Dunkirk] in 1689. [XEBR.6.11.1689]

WISO, a Fleming who settled in Upper Lanarkshire before 1200, at a site named Wiston. [SFP.50]

WOOD, ANDREW, was bound for Flanders in 1494. [ATS]

WOOD, DAVID, master of the Patience of Montrose from Montrose in Angus bound from Duinkerken [Dunkirk] in October 1681. [NRS.E72.16.13]

WOOD, ROBERT, master of the Bogfarla trading between Aberdeen and Vlaanderen [Flanders] in 1596. [ASW.25]

WOOD, ROBERT, a soldier of Lieutenant Colonel Sir Andrew Agnew's Company of the Scots Brigade, [De Schotse Brigade], in Brugge [Bruges] on 13 June 1745. [NRS.GD154.636]

WOOD, WILLIAM, master of the Three Swans arrived in Dundee on 26 April 1784 from Ostend. [NRS.E504.11.11]

WOTHERSPOON, MATTHEW, a merchant in Glasgow, trading with Brussels and Antwerp from 1829 to 1830. [NRS.CS96.446]

WRICHTON, THOMAS, a cramer from Aberdeen, was admitted as a burgess of Antwerpen [Antwerp] in 1544. [SA] [AB.398]

WRITER, THOMAS, [Thomas Wrichter], a citizen of Antwerp around 1540. [SA.Antwerpen, Poorterboek]

YOUNG, GEORGE, a Corporal of Lieutenant Colonel Sir Andrew Agnew's Company of the Scots Brigade, [De Schotse Brigade], in Brugge [Bruges] on 13 June 1745. [NRS.GD154.636]

YOUNG, JOHN, master of the Robert and John of Anstruther trading between Anstruther in Fife and Duinkerken [Dunkirk] in 1747-1749. [NRS.E504.3.1]

YOUNG, JOHN, master of the Sally of Perth trading between Perth and Duinkerken [Dunkirk] in 1764. NRS.E504.27.5]

YOUNG, M., a descriptive letter of a journey from Leiden via Veere, Middelburg, and places in Flanders and France to Saumur in 1654. [NRS.GD40.2.3.25]

YOUNG, ROBERT, master of the Christian of Montrose from Montrose to Duinkerken [Dunkirk] in March 1682. [NRS.E72.16.12]

YOUNG, ROBERT, a Captain of Colonel Graham's Regiment of Foot in [Vlaanderen] Flanders, husband of Helen Wauchope, testament, 29 March 1694, Commissariat of Edinburgh. [NRS]

YOUNG, THOMAS, master of the Newcastle Packet of Crail in Fife arrived in Anstruther in Fife in November 1742 from Duinkerken. [Dunkirk]. [NRS.E504.3.1]

YOUNG, WILLIAM, a Corporal of Captain Marjoribanks' Company of the Scots Brigade, [De Schotse Brigade], married Catherine Russell, daughter of the late Sergeant Russell, in Yperen [Ypres] on 20 April 1717. [SB]

YOUNG, ..., master of the whaler Raith of Leith was captured off the Shetland Islands on the return voyage from Greenland by a French privateer and taken to Dunkirk in 1794. [PL.296]

YOUNGER, HENRY, born 1605, a soldier who was granted a pass to travel to Flanders on 15 April 1635. [TNA.E157.20]

YUNGAR, WILLEM, a cordiner in Edinburgh in 1573. [SFP.66]

ZAN, STON, a Fleming, versus John Cant, before the Admiralty Court in Edinburgh in February 1558. [ACB.87/100/119]

Some early Flemish Emigrants to the New Netherlands

DE LA WARDE, JAN, from Antwerpen, was aboard the De Vos master Jacob Jansz. Huys, was bound to the New Netherlands on 31 August 1662. [N.Y.Col.Docs.xiii]

DIRCKSEN, ANTHONY, from Brabant, was aboard the De Vos master Jacob Jansz. Huys, was bound to the New Netherlands on 31 August 1662. [N.Y.Col.Docs.xiii]

ENJART, CAREL, with his wife and three children, from Flanders, were aboard the De Eendracht, master Jan Bergen, bound for the New Netherlands on 17 April 1664. [N.Y.Col.Docs.xiii]

HOOPELYNE, JOOST, with his wife and son, from Flanders, were aboard De Bonte Koe, master Jan Bergen, bound for the New Netherlands on 16 April 1663. [N.Y.Col.Docs.xiii]

HOOPELYNE, JOOST, the younger, with his wife and child, from Flanders, were aboard De Bonte Koe, master Jan Bergen, bound for the New Netherlands on 16 April 1663. [N.Y.Col.Docs.xiii]

JURIAENSZ., JENNEKEN, from Grevekeur in Brabant, was aboard De Trouw, master Jan Jaisz. Bestevaer, bound for the New Netherlands on 20 January 1664. [N.Y.Col.Docs.xiii]

KOCHRIJT, JOOST, a soldier from Brugge, bound for the New Netherlands aboard the Otter on 27 April 1660. [N.Y.Col.Docs.xiii]

LUTEN, WILRAVEN, with his wife and child, from Flanders, were bound for the New Netherlands aboard the De Jan Baptist, master Jan Bergen, on 9 May 1661. [N.Y.Col.Docs.xiii]

PAULUSSEN, GOMMERT, from Antwerpen, was bound for the New Netherlands aboard the De Jan Baptist, master Jan Bergen, on 9 May 1661. [N.Y.Col.Docs. xiii]

WILLAYS, FERDANDUS, a soldier from Kortrjk, bound for the New Netherlands aboard the Otter on 27 April 1660. [N.Y.Col.Docs.xiii]

www.ingramcontent.com/pod-product-compliance
Lightning Source LLC
Chambersburg PA
CBHW061959220426
43662CB00011B/1742